FIRST PRINTING

Library of Congress Catalog Card Number: 66-18519

Distributed by Dodd, Mead & Company, New York

5 North Wabash Avenue, Chicago, Illinois 60602

Printed in the U.S.A.

SELL YOURSELF BIG

by

Edwin A. Moll

DEDICATION

To my wife, Natalie

Acknowledgements

"A friend is one to whom we may pour out the contents of our hearts, chaff and grain together, knowing that the gentlest of hands will sift it, keep what is worth keeping, and with a breath of kindness, blow the rest away."

I acknowledge with deep appreciation the following friends:

Dr. George Connelly
Maggie Daly
Benny Dunn
Dorothy Hopkins
Mitchell Leikin
Herb Lyon
Col. Mel Mawrence
Roy P. Stealey
Martin Topaz
Peter M. Topaz
Marvyn Wittelle

TABLE OF CONTENTS

TABLE OF CONTENTS

PREFACE

Have you ever gotten that feeling that life is like playing a game of musical chairs? Those days when the work piles up, yet you still have to spend time with your family and outside activities—club meetings, church and social affairs—your life reaches a point where you are frantically switching from one activity to another. If you fit into this whirlwind picture, and most of us do, then you should have little trouble understanding and utilizing the underlying concept of SELL YOURSELF BIG.

Everyone's life is composed of dozens of varying activities. Sociologists have "dubbed" these various activities with the name "roles." An individual plays many roles. For example, a man might be a doctor by profession; he may also be a husband and a father, belong to a fraternal organization, be a member of a professional association, a member of a social group, a church member, be a member of the local P.T.A., active in a community political organization and be a patron of the arts. Each of these activities is a separate "role." Even though the man playing these roles is the same man, he presents himself differently in each situation; his personality changes depending on his involvement with his current role.

As you go along in your daily life, you are constantly changing from one role to another; sociologists call this concept *role switching*, and it is a necessary part of everyone's life.

SELL YOURSELF BIG is designed to help you present yourself in a better light in most of the roles with which you may find yourself involved.

Organized into three basic areas, SELL YOURSELF BIG presents: 1. The philosophies and techniques of Administrative Public Relations; 2. Public relations methods for you to use in your earning capacity; and 3. Public relations practices that you may find useful in your outside activities.

Before you read this book you should study the Table of Contents and decide which chapters apply to your many roles. The chapters on history, mechanics of publicity, dangers of public relations and the use of creativity in public relations are of universal interest and should be read by everyone.

By the way, reading chapters which are not directly related to you, may provide some new ideas that can be adapted to your own activities or give you new areas of interest.

Mr. Moll's concept of Administrative Public Relations is an exciting new approach to an old method. A perceptive man once said, ". . . public relations is 90 per cent doing good, and 10 per cent telling about it." Mr. Moll expands this basic premise into a developmental theory of public relations for the individual. It is not necessary to have a million dollar public relations budget to utilize this book, nor is it necessary to have your own public relations counsel. SELL YOURSELF BIG is written for the individual who wants to learn how to do his own public relations and to present a better image of himself in public and in private life.

By learning Mr. Moll's concepts of Administrative Public Relations and following his advice and programs, we feel that SELL YOURSELF BIG will prove to be financially, as well as personally, rewarding to you.

PETER M. TOPAZ
Publisher

Mr. Moll and the late President John F. Kennedy.

FOREWORD

As I write this foreword for Ed Moll's book, SELL YOURSELF BIG, I suddenly realize that I am at the age where I wish a book like this had been available to me 30 years ago.

I have many "hats" in my career . . . television . . . lecturing . . . writing books . . . and finally and most happily . . . writing a column for one of our major metropolitan newspapers, "Chicago's American." I have loved every facet of my work.

My daily activities as wage earner, wife, mother, columnist and participant in civic affairs, have

Governor Otto Kerner of Illinois appears on a radio program with Edwin A. Moll.

placed me in many roles—all of which have been rewarding even though they were demanding.

However, the lack of adequate guidelines has sometimes made it extremely difficult to adjust to these various roles. I know now that if there had been a blueprint like this book, throughout my career, I would have found my life much less complicated.

My confidence in Ed Moll is based upon the fact that his very sound philosophy of life and of business has led him to a great deal of personal success. He was involved in Chicago politics at the age of 14 as a precinct captain (the youngest in America) . . . at 16, he was the vice-president of a cosmetic company . . . at 20, he owned and operated three restaurants . . . at 22, he was business manager for Chicago's Adler Planetarium . . . and at the ripe age of 24, he was an aide to Chicago's Mayor Richard J. Daley.

Senator Stuart Symington (D-Mo.), former secretary of the air force, discusses his views of United States military preparedness.

Mr. Moll, too, wears many "hats." His services as a public relations counsel are much in demand. Yet, his "hats" are so well placed and organized that he is able to devote time to such activities as producing and moderating radio programs, politics, public service and youth welfare programs.

As a commissioner of Youth Welfare for a Chicago suburb, a local chairman of the Red Cross and Community Fund drives, special events director of a Chicago radio station, administrative direc-

Adlai E. Stevenson, former governor of Illinois and ambassador to the United Nations, is escorted by Edwin A. Moll during a campaign tour through Chicago.

tor of an association, and Midwest director of Asthmacade, it is obvious that Mr. Moll is qualified to write a book of this nature. He has had actual experience in the art of "Selling oneself big."

For 20 years, I have been exposed to the people, philosophies and techniques involved in public relations. I have found that all too often overlooked are the small businessman, the professional practitioner, the small town chamber of commerce, and millions of others who cannot afford the luxury of hiring outside public relations counsels.

Maggie Daly

SELL YOURSELF BIG has corrected these omissions. Ed Moll has included chapters on history, mechanics and the dangers of public relations; he has maintained the proper perspective. He wanted to write a book that would provide concrete suggestions and specific courses of action for those who needed them most. And I think he has succeeded.

Remember: no matter what you do or say . . . your public relations are showing. SELL YOURSELF BIG will help you show them off to your own best advantage.

MAGGIE DALY
Columnist
"Chicago's American"

G. Mennen "Soapy" Williams, former governor of Michigan; Edwin A. Moll; and Richard J. Daley, mayor of Chicago.

Pointing out the city's highlights, Edwin A. Moll conducts Huh Chung, then acting President of South Korea, on a tour of Chicago.

BALLOON
SYB

HISTORY

When Ur stepped out of his cave, met Ud, and said, "ugh," public relations was born. For from the manner, expression, and intonation of the greeting Ud was able to form an opinion about Ur—and that is the essence of public relations. Of course, neither of them knew this. It happened well over 50,000 years ago, there was no public, and neither of these two gentlemen knew anything about relations, or even any word for it. Until that very day, all communications between humans had been by signal only.

Nearly 40,000 years were to pass before people had any formal means of communication, other than by a slowly evolving spoken language. Then some man, or woman, began to draw crude pictures on the walls of the cave in which he lived. Those pictures told others what he had seen, how he lived, and, perhaps, even what he was thinking. The earliest forms of writing were not to be invented for another seven thousand years.

And Civilization Was Born

In the meantime men had begun to live together; principally for protection, partly for sharing provisions, and partly for companionship. This was primarily family life; the sons and daughters of one family, along with their wives, husbands and children and perhaps a few aunts, uncles and grandparents included, formed the community.

Then an epochal event occurred. Man learned, by accident or reason, that by using the waters of rivers for irrigation, he could plant, raise and control his own food supply. Under rugged, primitive conditions this required concentrated effort and constant work. It could be accomplished best by cooperative effort between the people of more than one family commune. So people gathered together in small villages—and Civilization was born.

The advent of civilization brought with it a significant concomitant. If people were to live and work together, someone had to lead the way while the others were willing to follow. More important, it was imperative that the leader should be able to persuade the others that he was their leader, that he knew what should be done, that they knew he knew and would obey his directives. The leaders, in other words, recognized that there was a necessity for planned interrelationships.

Follow The Leader

To secure their positions of authority, these men took it upon themselves to interpret for the rest of the populace the words and wishes of the gods. Now, man himself had created these gods: the wind, the water, the fire, storm, sun, rain, and any other natural occurrence that he could not comprehend. For the most part, each citizen of these earliest civilizations was content to follow the lead of someone who, he believed, could talk with these gods. Particularly would he do so as long as he could be assured of a place to live, have enough to eat, and be able to communicate with the gods that controlled his life. Religion, in other words, while fostered by fear and a desire to avoid the dangers from, and curry the favor of, the gods, was born a brother to civilization.

Before long, the specialization which was an integral part of civilization had created three distinct classes of citizens. At the bottom of the scale were the farmers, the growers of the grain which fed the entire populace. At the top were the priests, the autocratic rulers who interpreted the wishes of the gods. And standing in the middle were the soldiers, a special class of bodyguards, personal servants and enforcers which the priests had created to maintain their rule in case the words of the gods were insufficient. With a growing fighting group in command, the priests were soon in a position to seek out and conquer other nearby villages and to enslave their populations—thus creating a fourth class. And with this same fighting group the religious leaders were able to enforce their demands and commands upon their own citizenry.

Affecting Public Opinion

The leaders of these first theocratic civilizations were aware of the three main elements of community life: informing people, persuading people, and integrating people with people. While they had their soldiers with whom they could enforce all three measures, they also resorted to methods which individuals would accept much more quiescently: magic, taboo and superstition. Some of these hundreds of centuries old devices, particularly superstitions, are used today by so-called civilized people who want to implement their greed and extend their own power or influence.

With the growth of the size of individual civilizations to include thousands, then tens of thousands, and finally hundreds of thousands of people, a form of secular leadership arose. Powerful military men, using the armies of soldiers as enforcers, proclaimed themselves kings or emperors. The priests were reduced to religious leadership, merely one step above the farmer and merchant citizens. Since few, if any, of the populace had occasion to see, or deal with, the king, it became increasingly important for him to impress his greatness and power upon them—for it was from the citizenry that the ruler accumulated his wealth. The tombs and temples, the writings and records which have since been unearthed bear witness to the huge sums of time, money and ingenuity that were spent in this effort. Some rulers went so far as to proclaim themselves gods, and to have statues in their images and temples to their sanctity erected at which the people could worship and pay their respects. These men were engaged in affecting opinion in their way just as much as today's public relations counselors use modern methods of communication for the same purpose.

The invention of writing, sometime before the 16th Century B.C., was a significant step in changing the methods of persuasion open to the rulers. They could now communicate their wishes by way of the written word. What they wrote could become law, open to the interpretation of those who were in power, and to be used for good or for evil. The publication of the Bible, handwritten of course, meant that the word of God could be disseminated amongst His followers. And while the ancient Hebrew prophets, unlike the kings and emperors of other nations, considered themselves mere humans, no different than their followers, they were still able to command respect and a measure of obedience by interpreting the Laws of the Lord to the people.

A Two-Way Street

Epochal in the history of civilization and the molding of opinion, was the achievement, in Greece, of a democratic way of life. The individual now became important, achieved a sense of personality. This meant that his opinion, combined with the opinions of his fellow citizens, contributed to the way he was ruled and allowed to live. An interrelationship arose between people and people, groups and groups, leaders and followers. Opinion on all matters, in other words, had now become a two-way street.

While the actual concept of public opinion stemmed from the ancient Greeks, it was the Romans who finally brought it to full flowering. They not only recognized, but gave voice to this great *fait accompli.* It was in Rome that such phrases as *vox populi,* the Voice of the People, *res publicae,* public affairs, and *rumores,* rumors, were first used and given credence. Julius Caesar even went so far as to have a handwritten daily newspaper circulated in Rome so the people would know what their government was doing, and what was expected of them.[1] For a few short centuries it seemed that this two-way street of opinion was to become the way of the world. But, in 475 A.D., barbarous Germanic tribes over-ran the Roman Empire. With their coming, all free exchange of public opinion was suspended. The Dark Ages descended on Europe and none but a very few rulers could speak out or establish any laws. So-called free citizens and slaves alike were forced to submit to an unchanging, harsh status quo in which only the decrees of the rulers were important. In Europe the Pope, through the Church, was the undisputed leader who neither asked nor accepted any opinions or ideas from the people and demanded absolute allegiance and obedience. The military establishment, under the control of the Church, ruthlessly enforced these measures.

Things Began To Move

It was only after seven or eight centuries of darkness and quiet that a restlessness manifested itself in England. Separated from the continent by the English Channel, the people there could not quite so readily be controlled by the Church in Rome. Dissatisfaction grew and outcries became louder until, in the year 1215, the common man leaped into prominence by forcing on King John the Magna Charta. This historic document, by guaranteeing freedoms and independence, became the foundation upon which were built freedom of expression, persuasion and open, vocalized differences of opinion.

Shortly thereafter, rumblings began to be heard on the continent itself. Experiments in new forms of art began to appear, at first surreptitiously, and

Note: All quotation from, or reference to, Bernays are from: Edward L. Bernays, *Public Relations* (Norman, Oklahoma: University of Oklahoma Press, 1952). Similar references to Goldman are from: Eric F. Goldman, *Two-Way Street, The Emergence of the Public Relations Counsel* (Cambridge, Massachusetts: Bellman Publishing Company, Inc., 1948).

[1]Bernays—p. 16

King John signing the Magna Carta.

Historical Picture Service Photo

then openly, in the 14th Century. Then things really began to move. Sometime in the middle of the 15th Century came what might be termed the fourth epochal event in civilization's history—the invention of movable type. Now, for the first time, the written word could be disseminated widely and relatively quickly. With it opinion did not have to rely on word of mouth or laboriously hand-written tracts. Thousands could now be persuaded at one time.

Thus, with one brilliant stroke, man broke the chains that had bound him to silence and ignorance for eight centuries. The Rennaissance, ". . . a secular movement that stressed the rights of reason to investigate nature and society"[2] rapidly came to a head. On its heels, led by the brilliant Martin Luther, came the Reformation, ". . . a religious movement that stressed the rights of individual con-

[2]Bernays—p. 17

science."[3] Man was now free to move forward by the open interchange of idea and opinion. It is significant to note that without the Rennaissance and the Reformation, today's "public relations" would have been impossible.

So rapidly did the fires of the new freedom spread that by 1575 Gregory XIII established the Committee for the Propagation of the Faith. This simple defensive act on the part of the Church introduced into the language a new word, and one of the most powerful weapons ever to be put into the hands of mankind—"Propaganda." From that day to this, propaganda has played a significant role in every step, forward or backward, taken by the community of man. People of authority and intelligence were beginning to recognize, in a vague sort of way, the power that opinion of the masses could exert.

First Printed Daily in 1615

The first regularly published newsletter was initiated in 1609 in Augsburg, Germany. This was followed quickly by the first daily newspaper in 1615 in Frankfurt. It is perhaps ironical that the country that first pushed man into eight centuries of bitter blackness, should also be one of the first to spawn the seeds of the great power of man's freedom. The first English language daily newspaper appeared in 1622. At the same time two other symposiums were gathering wide-spread prominence—the French Salon and the English Coffee House. Both were gathering places where politicians, writers and ordinary citizens congregated to exchange ideas and opinions. Now, truly, man had disencumbered himself, and despite the last ditch efforts of some demagogic religious and secular leaders, he was free to express himself. Public opinion has become a major force in western civilization.

It was this same public opinion, in the form of more than thirty thousand political pamphlets and newspapers, that led directly to the Puritan Revolution in the 17th Century England. And it was

[3] *Ibid.*

this same public opinion which, in the latter part of the same century, in skilled minds, began planting the seeds of the American Revolution. As early as 1681, Pennsylvania publicly proclaimed freedom of opinion as a human right.[4] Fourteen years later, England, through public pressure, abolished licensing of the press. Now, at least in England and her colonies, everyone was free not only to talk about, but to print, anything he chose. France, much slower to accept the new freedoms, saddled with a gilded monarchy and a lowly peasantry, was not to abolish such licensing until almost a century later.[5]

Publicizing a Tea Party

It was under these favorable circumstances, early in the 18th Century, that the visionaries and revolutionists began to plot the final demise of tyranny in the English-speaking world. American radicals of that day began to use every device available to them to gain support for their independence. Oratory, newspapers, meetings, committees, pamphlets and public and private correspondence began to flood the colony. A great proportion of everything that was written in America at that time had to do with the idea of independence. In 1732 Benjamin Franklin established the first subscription library in the world—a new method of disseminating information to the public.[6] About the same time Samuel Adams, who has been called the "Father of the American Revolution," began to develop techniques of influence that are still in use today. His vision, and his ideas, were so inflammatory, so novel and so effective that they soon began to affect a large and influential segment of the populace. A. M. Lee, one of the few historians of public relations, has termed him "The Father of American Press Agentry."

---

[4]Bernays—p. 28

[5]Indeed, there are countries in the world where censorship, licensing, and a fearful inhibition of public opinion are still maintained by dictatorial governments.

[6]Bernays—p. 22

Perhaps the first overt act of public relations in history was the famous Boston Tea Party. Contrary to much popular belief, this famed maneuver was no spontaneous raid. It was carefully staged to dramatize the American resistance movement. And Samuel Adams, quick to recognize its value to his cause, saw to it that the details were widely publicized. Paul Revere was one of the men who carried its message throughout the New England area.

A Sense of Public Relationships

The result of all this action, pressure and publicity was, of course, the Declaration of Independence, which is still, next to the Bible, the most widely known and recognized piece of literature in the western world. Proof that the Declaration of Independence was devised as a molder of public opinion, as a public relations "stunt" in effect, is available in the words of Thomas Jefferson himself: "When forced, therefore, to resort to arms for redress, an appeal to the tribunal of the world was deemed proper for our justification. This was the object of the Declaration of Independence." Today, almost exactly the same words are being used freely, before the United Nations and in many individual countries, to promulgate the reasons for many overt acts of unilateral decision. Obviously, the Americans could have fought England for freedom without such a document. Obviously, too, American patriots like Jefferson thought that one was necessary to win the support of the rest of the world. Edward L. Bernays says that Jefferson's statement summed up "that sense of Public Relationships which inhere in true public relations."[7]

The final stamp of approval was placed upon the rights of people everywhere to express themselves and their opinions freely by the American Bill of Rights—added to our Constitution in 1791.

With all of this action, secret and overt, express and implied, and with all of the techniques that

---

[7]*Ibid.*—p. 34

The Boston Tea Party.

Historical Picture Service Photo

were developed to influence and mold the thinking of men everywhere, we do not actually find the term "public opinion" used until about the time of the French Revolution, just prior to 1789. However, it did gain enough prominence in a short time that William Pitt, the English Prime Minister, termed the French Revolution "armed opinion." This same revolt also brought with it the first official governmental recognition of the importance of the wishes of the public. In 1792 the French National Assembly established, as a section of the Ministry of the Interior, the *Bureau d'Esprit*, the Bureau of Spirit. It was the duty of this department to keep the public informed about what its government was doing, and also to keep the government informed of the desires and movements of the citizenry. Shades of Julius Caesar, raised after fifteen hundred years!

"Armed Opinion"

And so closed the century, which, because of the fantastic strides that had been made in the spread of opinion and discussion, was called "The Age of Enlightenment." From this point on, our history will consider only the growth of public relations in the United States, where its development, at least for commercial purposes, has far surpassed that of any other nation.[8]

With the opening of the 19th Century, "public relations," a phrase which had not yet been uttered, entered an interim period. For more than a hundred years it was to have neither the spontaneous enthusiasm which had led, in the last half of the previous century, to two tremendous political revolutions, nor the magnificent changes in spirit and techniques which were to mark the first half of the next. Yet it was not a dull period. Several significant advances in the technology of communications, a gradual awakening of public spirited thinking, and a host of emotion-packed issues were to keep it moving forward inexorably.

Leaping Communications

Inherent in the spread of public information was the development of better and faster means of communication. Four significant inventions were to play important roles in this phase of history. The first steam railroad was invented in the United States in 1829. Then, following more than 200 years of experimentation with various forms of telegraphy by scientists from many countries, Samuel Morse developed his system in 1835. Forty-one years later Alexander Graham Bell completed the first telephonic conversation in the world. These three inventions all spread rapidly, giving great impetus

---

[8]It should be noted, however, that in recent years, public relations, or propaganda by government agencies, has been used much more effectively by countries such as England, Germany and Russia than by our own.

to the rapid dissemination of communications of all kinds. Finally, following an orderly system of experiments and development by various scientists, here and abroad, the first purely radio transmission was introduced by Marconi in 1895. This first signal covered one mile. The next year the distance was increased to nine miles. In 1898 radio waves were covering 74 miles, and by 1900 had reached 200 miles. Then, in 1901 radio leaped the Atlantic Ocean with the first Transatlantic broadcast covering 2000 miles.

Offer additional services

Though technical advancements were important, the issues, emotions of the day, plus new techniques for molding public opinion were of much greater significance to the development of public relations.

The period of 1800 to 1865 was marked by many conflicts. Differences erupted between the commercial East and the pioneering West, between industry and agriculture, between the traditional values propounded originally by Alexander Hamilton and those favored by Thomas Jefferson and Andrew Jackson, by the fights over annexation of new territory and by one of the most hotly debated issues of the day—Manifest Destiny. But the one truly great, and certainly the most emotional, issue of the period was slavery. As the people took sides on these various issues, techniques and methods of influence changed with the times and with the developing ideas.

The early 1800s were marked by the rise of the "Penny Press"—newspapers which, because they drew their principal revenue from advertising, could be sold en masse for one penny per copy. Because the income of these papers depended upon advertisers, merchants and manufacturers were able, to a great degree, to control what appeared in the papers. "Free Puffs," advertising that was published as news, became the rule. Both the news and editorial columns of all the papers were filled with in-

P. T. BARNUM'S

New and Only Greatest Show on Earth.

IN WATER-PROOF TENTS, COVERING SEVERAL ACRES. $1,000,000 INVESTED.

A GREAT AND AMUSING ACADEMY OF OBJECT TEACHING.

Musenm, Menagerie, Circus, and Hippodrome.

Will travel by rail, on 100 Steel Cars of its own, passing through New York, the Canadas, Michigan, Illinois, Minnesota, Wisconsin, Indiana, Iowa, Missouri, and Texas. The Museum contains 100,000 rare and startling curiosities, including the most remarkable Captain COSTENTENUS, a Greek nobleman, who was

TATTOED FROM HEAD TO FOOT

in Chinese Tartary, as punishment for engaging in rebellion against the King.

The **MENAGERIE** consists of by far the largest collection of living wild animals that ever travelled, among which are the $25,000 Hippopotamus from the river Nile, Sea Lions from Alaska, Giraffes, the African Lioness and her little royal Cubs, no larger than cats, a picture of which occupies a full page in HARPER'S WEEKLY of April 28th. The six beautiful jet-black $30,000 Trakene Stallions, from Paris, present amazing and ENTIRELY NOVEL performances, which have been witnessed with delight by over 200,000 ladies, gentlemen, and children this spring at Barnum's great Hippodrome Building in New York. This picture shows them

EXACTLY AS THEY APPEAR IN THE RING,

where also will appear twice each day one hundred peerless performers, funny clowns, and more than a hundred beautiful Arabian horses, ponies, elephants, camels, and other marvelously-educated performing animals. A Golden Street Procession a mile in length, full of startling features, with immense glittering Chariots, men in Armor, Bands of Music, curious Automatons, OPEN CAGES OF LIONS, in which AN INTREPID LADY PERFORMER APPEARS, and ENORMOUS SERPENTS, with their FEARLESS KEEPERS INSIDE THE CAGES, takes place daily from 9 to 10 o'clock A.M.

Cheap excursion trains, conveying passengers to the town where the exhibition takes place.

Historical Picture Service Photo

The first of the great publicists was P. T. Barnum.

formation beneficial to the advertiser and frequently inimical to the public interest.

Such practices brought to the fore the first great American Press Agents. In 1840 Phineas T. Barnum announced that he had discovered an old

Negro slave who had nursed George Washington some one hundred years before—one Joice Heth. Barnum exhibited Joice Heth to the public for a fee. The furor raised by this claim became nationwide. Countless letters were published by all of the great papers on both sides of the issue. Some praised the promoter for bringing forth this human relic. It is probably safe to assume that these were the papers in which Barnum placed his advertising. However, just as many were vitriolic in their condemnation of the exploitation of an unknowing slave. In reality the greatest unknowing people were the public. Most of the letters, on both sides of the issue, were written by Barnum himself. When Joice Heth died, doctors who examined her claimed she could not have been over eighty years of age and therefore not even alive when Washington was born. True to his methods, Barnum declared himself shocked and publicly stated that he himself had been taken in. Nevertheless, the indefatigable agent was just beginning. Over the next years he successfully promoted General Tom Thumb, Jenny Lind—"The Swedish Nightingale," "Zip, the What Is It," the Cardiff Giant, an obvious hoax, and finally, in his waning years, "The Greatest Show on Earth"—the great circus which eventually became an American institution.

Greatest Show on Earth

Barnum, of course, was not alone in taking advantage of an unsophisticated public avid for news of any kind. Men such as Washington Irving, Lyman Beecher and William Watson were using the public and private press of the country to promote their own interests. Horace Greeley probably had more to do with starting the Civil War than any other individual in the country.

In The Public Interest

And yet, through it all, a few conscientious people were beginning to be worried. They could see the great harm that could accrue to a gullible public if these practices were to be perpetuated. In 1827, for instance, the Reverend O. P. Hoyt was quoted as emphasizing "correct" public opinion as "the safeguard of socially desirable institutions."[9] And in 1842 Hugh Smith, Rector of St. Peter's Church of New York city, in a talk to the alumni of Columbia University, used the term "Public Relations."[10] It is the first recorded use of the term and the Reverend Smith used it to refer to things that would be in the public interest. Then, in 1848, the New York Herald announced that it would no longer disguise paid advertising as editorial matter. These were among the first conscientious efforts to put an end to the centuries during which ". . . the press agent operated on the principle of the public be fooled."[11]

In the meantime techniques were improving.

Lincoln understood public opinion

Abraham Lincoln, who was wise enough to recognize that ". . . with public sentiment nothing can fail; without it, nothing can succeed," understood, perhaps more than any other man of his time, the effect of public opinion and the way to use it. During the entire 1864 Presidential campaign, he almost remained silent. Throughout the entire months of the campaign, his managers and boosters were traversing the country, pleading his cause and using only arguments that would appeal to the particular audience to which they might be talking. Slavery was only one issue of the time and was stressed only in sections of the country where the abolitionist feeling ran high. In areas where the slavery issue was weak, his agents used other arguments: Carl Schurz appealed to labor and the German vote; protective tariffs were preached in the iron and steel areas; in the North and West the people were given "Manifest Destiny" and the inevitable struggle betwen the U.S. and Russia to think about. Further, once the war had started, he could talk, in all honesty, of the need for ". . . sound and conscious engineering of public opinion here

---

[9]Goldman—p. 2
[10]Bernays—p. 46
[11]Goldman—p. 1

and abroad in the interests of the Union."[12] Such a statement was cast in the same mold as that of Thomas Jefferson's concerning the need for the Declaration of Independence almost one hundred years before.

Following the Civil War, large scale commerce and industry became the dominant factor in the economic and political life of the country. The "Robber Barons," as the leaders of these new industries came to be called, believed that their methods of operation should be kept absolutely secret. Their ethics, goals, and the manner of achieving them were considered sacrosanct and they would not allow the public or the government to know one word about them. Professor N.S.B. Gras actually traces this history of secrecy in business back to the medieval guilds. The public, too, seemed to acquiesce to this policy of secrecy. The United States was in the midst of the period of *Laissez Faire*, when it was right and fair for business to grow in any way that it could. The "Almighty Dollar" had become the standard of the people and the goal of business.

"The Public Be Damned"

Then in 1879 a bombshell was dropped on the American public. Commodore William Vanderbilt of the New York Central Railroad, asked by a reporter how his rescheduling of certain trains would affect the public, answered, "The public be damned!"[13]

For several years railroad magnates had been waging open warfare upon each other and upon other industries. This conflict finally reached dertimental, and sometimes violent, proportions that antagonisms on the part of the public were inevitable. Vanderbilt's blasphemy was the catalyst that brought the reaction out into the open.

---

[12]Bernays—p. 36

[13]While there are several versions of how this came about, everyone has Vanderbilt giving the same response in answer to a question by a newspaper reporter.

The first counter-reaction came from groups who felt the squeeze most: the working man, the farmer-voter of the Midwest, and the Eastern intellectual. In 1882, lawyer Dorman Eaton called for public relations by all groups, interpreting the term as actions to be used for the public good.[14] And in 1883, the noted journalist Joseph Pulitzer, urging that the public be kept informed, stated, "There is not a crime, a dodge, not a trick, not a swindle, not a vice, which does not live by secrecy. Get these things out in the open . . . and sooner or later public opinion will sweep them away." That statement, as true today as the day it was made, should be constantly in the mind of every person or group that would court public favor.

Crime Feeds on Secrecy

Along with the reaction to Vanderbilt and the Robber Barons came further evidence of the growing integrity of a few people in the publishing business. In 1888, before the American Newspaper Publishers convention, J. E. McManus of the Philadelphia Record read a paper on "Puffs and the Dividing Line between News and Advertising." Despite the fact that the real effort to eliminate this subterfuge did not come about for another twenty years, the close of the 19th Century was ". . . marked by an increasing development of public relations techniques by (various) pressure groups."[15]

The public reaction, in the 1880s, to the secrecy of business plus the restless awakening of the public mind to the inequities that such procedures had spawned, plus the "trust busting" efforts of President Theodore Roosevelt, led, in the early 1900s, to the rise of a new breed of public opinion molders. Roosevelt, himself, coined the word to describe these practitioners, who, like a character in *Pilgrim's Progress*, "could look no way but downward with the muckrake in his hands." Thus 1903 to 1909 was the time of the infamous "Muckrakers."

[14]Goldman—p. 2 [15]Bernays—p. 61

Despised by Both Sides

This small group of men, reporters and writers, reviled American business, American politics, and everything and everyone who did not agree with them. They sought and exposed every issue that could be used to stir emotions and build circulation. They were the leeches who clung to the journalistic coat-tails of leaders who were raising public opinion against the charlatans, the defrauders and the cheaters of their day. They were despised by both sides: the businessmen and politicians they degraded, as well as by the real liberal leaders who were fighting the same people, but using a clean pen.

In 1902 a young man named Ivy Lee was working as a financial reporter for the New York Journal. In his mind a new idea was being formed. If the muckrakers could use publicity, as it was called then, to smear business, why not use this same tool to explain and defend business. In 1903 Ivy Lee quit his job and entered publicity work exclusively.

During his time with the Journal, Lee had had the opportunity to watch developments in the damaging and bitter anthracite coal strike of 1902. He saw the mine owners refuse any cooperation at all . . . to the press, the public or the miners. And he watched John Mitchell lead the miners in a campaign of full cooperation. News conferences were held regularly. Reams of news stories were supplied to the press. Any and all cooperation was offered to the mine owners as well as to the public and the government. Ivy Lee was fascinated as he saw the deluge of publicity turn public opinion to the side of the miners—and the great victory it won for their cause.

Something the Public Approves

In 1906 another, and greater, strike developed against these same anthracite mine owners. By this time, however, the owners had learned their lesson. They immediately hired Parker and Lee, the publicity firm that Lee started. Lee advised the owners that this time they must cooperate fully with all media and that the public must "be informed." This statement became the cornerstone of public communications during the early 1900s.

Even though big business was finally beginning to realize that the public could no longer be damned or ignored, Lee's active mind kept one step ahead. He realized that if publicity was to win favor, mere information was not enough; it had to contain something that the public thought was good.[16] This recognition led him, inevitably, to the next step. If publicity must contain something that the public approved, then the public must be interpreted to the business. The entrepreneur and tycoon had to know what the public would like if they were to win its favor.

Publicity for the public good

Throughout this first decade of the century many prominent people were exerting pressure on business and opinion. William Graham Sumner, William James, Jane Addams, William Dean Howells, Mark Twain, Thomas Wentworth Higginson are just a few of the names that have gone down in history as having contributed to the general uplifting of the period. It was practically as a result of the teachings and preachings of such people that business—big business—finally began to recognize and accept the fact that favorable public opinion was vital to its continued existence and growth.

In 1908, T. N. Vail, president of American Telephone and Telegraph Company, used the term "public relations" and referred to it as an asset for his company.[17] Then, again in 1913, Vail stated for his company: "We have found . . . that our interests were best served when the public interests were best served." In 1916, Ivy Lee, still in the forefront, conceived the idea that good publicity involved doing as well as saying.

As pointed out earlier, Abraham Lincoln had well understood the mood of the public and the benefit

---

[16]Goldman—p. 9

[17]Bernays—p. 70

The Power of Propaganda

of appealing to it. However, the first Presidents of our country to use publicity actively for specific purposes were Theodore Roosevelt and Woodrow Wilson. Roosevelt's Anti-Trust actions could not have succeeded without widespread popular appeal, and Wilson used every technique known at the time to sell his "New Freedom" to the people.

As a matter of fact, from 1914 to 1918, the United States Government was the number one factor in public relations in the country.[18] Every known device of persuasion and suggestion was used to sell our war aims and ideas at home and abroad, as well as to deflate the people and abilities of our enemies. On April 6, 1917, just one week after we declared war on Germany, Wilson set up the Committee on Public Information under the direction of George Creel, a leading publicist of the day. Throughout the war this committee, and every other branch of the government, used publicity to further the needs of the individual departments as well as to build mountainous patriotic fervor. Liberty Bond sales, the welfare of the "Doughboy," love for our allies and hatred of our enemies all felt the powerful touch of public opinion as molded by the deliberate machinery of publicity. Indeed, several years later, it was Roger Babson, the business sage, who summed up the results of wartime publicity by stating that "The war taught us the power of propaganda."

It is interesting to note that despite the fact that private molding of public opinion had been going on for several centuries, hardly a word had been written about the process or the fact. As late as 1915 *Book Review Digest* had no listings at all under "publicity" or "public opinion." "Under the headings, public opinion, public relations, and publicity, the New York Public Library lists only eighteen items printed in all the years before 1917."[19] The first full book on the subject was not

[18] *Ibid.*—p. 71

[19] Goldman—p. 13

written until 1923, the same year that saw the introduction of the first public relations course ever offered by any school.

Castigating Press Agents

The end of the war opened the flood gates. Words, ideas, acts and facts poured forth in ever increasing volume. "Developments in the twenties reveal . . . public relations was a new field . . . (and that) business, education, and the press—were beginning to recognize this fact."[20] Yet, like all historical development, the path was not smooth and continuous. Acceptance swung back and forth, with differing ideas of publicity competing with each other. One group favored the typical propaganda popular during the nineties, another preferred "whitewashing" publicity, others believed in fostering the ideas of the "public be informed" philosophy of the first decade, and the newer techniques stimulated by the war.

As late as February 19, 1920, *Printer's Ink*, the leading magazine of the advertising industry, was still castigating "press agents" and their attempts to get free publicity. To this Edward L. Bernays, a leading exponent of the new credo and a former member of the Committee on Public Information during the war, answered, on February 26, 1920, "No honest publicity man undertakes . . . to promise the printing or appearance of his material. What the lawyer does for his client in the court of law, we do for our clients in the court of public opinion through the daily and periodical press."[21] In his book *Two-Way Street*, published in 1946, Eric F. Goldman sums up the emerging attitude of the twenties: "For centuries the press agent operated on the principle of the public be fooled; in the early 1900's a group . . . shifted the emphasis to the public be informed; in the 1920's, American public relations was summoned to the credo of the public be understood."[22]

[20] Bernays—p. 98
[21] Printer's Ink—Feb. 26, 1920
[22] Goldman—p. 1

Throughout the second decade of this century large companies began to employ public relations counsel and to appoint "good-will" vice-presidents, whose sole job was the new public relations function. In 1922, Col. Robert Stewart, chairman of the board of Standard Oil Company of Indiana, stated, "It is not enough to advertise a product . . . the Public ought to be acquainted with the honesty and high character of the institution back of the product." We had come a long way from the "Robber Barons" of fifty years earlier.

Finally, in 1923, the first book devoted exclusively to public relations, *Crystallizing Public Opinion*, was written by Bernays. The book contained a revelation, heretofore unthought of and unrecognized—that a public relations man had to be a student of psychology and sociology. In the same year Bernays was hired by New York University to teach the first public relations course offered by any American school.

Jolson in the White House

Then, in 1924, reaching back one hundred-fifty years to the Boston Tea Party, the first deliberately overt act of public relations, Bernays created the first of what he was to call the Overt Act Technique. Calvin Coolidge, running for re-election to the Presidency, was regarded as a cold, silent iceberg. Under Bernay's direction, Coolidge invited to the White House for breakfast such national idols as Al Jolson, the Dolly Sisters, Charlotte Greenwood and other stage and screen stars. A smashing success, this simple act, spread upon the pages of the nation's newspapers and magazines, made Coolidge seem warm and human. In the same year, the first commercial use of this technique was adopted. Procter and Gamble sponsored a nationwide soap sculpture contest for children. Thousands of children (and their parents) submitted entries. The contest was so successful that it became an annual event, continued for more than 30 years.

And so the development went on, and on, and on throughout the twenties. Businessmen, educators and publicists taught and exercised the new, up-to-date methods of public relations in an honest, forthright manner. A few businessmen still clung to the secrecy or the press agentry of earlier times; newspapers and periodicals of the era praised or castigated the emerging profession as they saw it. Nevertheless, public relations, as a legitimate business, had arrived on the American scene to stay. From here on it was merely a question of silencing the last critics and nurturing the infant into full manhood. The process was to take another 20 years—and even then a few "hard-headed" businessmen were to hold out against one hundred per cent acceptance.

On the Scene to Stay

In the United States of America, 1930 arrived with the shock waves of the horrendous stock market debacle still reverberating, with the first recognitions of the mammoth depression which was to follow, and with big business still firmly holding the reins of the country's economy, politics, communications and social action. Only a very few of the nation's most astute economists were aware that the depression, for the average blue collar worker, had, in fact, started as far back as 1926. During those last four years, working hours had been reduced in many plants, thousands of workers had been laid off in others, and the real income of the country had begun to decline significantly.*

The rapid and wild spread of the depression touched every American. Poverty became the way of the day, and with it came fear, frustration and

*Strangely enough, to this day a tremendous number of economists, businessmen and labor leaders are still not aware of this fact. Federal income tax statistics, then generally released only after five or six years, show that unemployment and partial employment had been steadily reducing the buying power of the country during these years. It was this, in the final analysis, that cut sales and earnings of industry to the point that brought about the stock market crash of October, 1929.

Fear, Frustration, Anger

anger. Banks failed, and with them went the life savings of millions of people. More millions were out of work, out of funds, out of hope. On many street corners and in many rooms there was open talk of revolution. Many fantastic, and some not-quite-so-fantastic, schemes to help the country were promulgated by the demagogues, crackpots, do-gooders, and some honest, practical people.

John Steinbeck's "The Grapes of Wrath" presented the problem of the social welfare of the people versus the social situation. In January, 1934, Dr. Francis E. Townsend, of California, proposed

Historical Picture Service Photo

that the government should pay $200 per month to every unemployed person over 60 years old and of good character. In the same year, Father Coughlin, in Detroit, founded the National Union for Social Justice and advocated nationalization of banks, utilities and all natural resources. In August of 1935 Louisiana's Senator Huey Long proposed a "vague scheme" for redistributing the wealth of the country so that every family could have an automobile and a radio. These and other plans gathered their backers. Some of them, picked up and refined by more sober minds, led to the establishment of such now-well-accepted acts as the Social Security Program and a graduated income tax.

Through the entire period, through all the grandiose plans, two important factors were at work. First, it was obvious that the people blamed business for the depression. Second, again in American History the voice of the people was ringing loud and clear. In 1932, for the first time since the war, the Republicans, blamed for being too close to business and for their *Laissez Faire* attitude, were swept out of office. A new breed of politician, under the Democratic banner of Franklin Roosevelt, were elected to office.

Engaged in Mammoth Struggle

Another, and, for our purposes, a far more significant factor was also at work. Business woke up. It realized that its bad image had to be dispelled and that the only way that could be done was through adequate public relations. Many business leaders recognized that: 1. They must adhere to the principle that private business must be in the public interest if they were to survive; 2. The public interest is a changing concept and business must be ready to change with it; 3. The place of business in the American way of life had to be sold to the public.[23] So a start was made. And in 1936 businessmen learned, the hard way for them, that they had not been successful. Franklin Roosevelt, the champion of the underdog, by now a demi-god to the little people of the country, was swept back into office with the greatest plurality in history. Republicans retained only a minute handful of offices across the country. Businessmen had to conclude that public relations had failed them, that the techniques were not yet sufficiently advanced to do the job, or that they had not tried hard enough. The next four years underscored their real belief: they had not yet really accepted and believed in what they were trying to do. Now they recognized that

[23]Bernays—p. 103

they were really engaged in a mammoth struggle for existence itself, and all the stops were out. Public relations men, those who were honest and knew their business, became not just another cog, but important staff members in industry.

American Public Growing Up

Now businessmen were ready to listen when H. A. Batten, president of N. W. Ayer & Son, advertising agency, said, "Any public relations worthy of the name must start with the business itself. Unless the business is so organized and so administered that it can meet at every point the test of good citizenship and of usefulness to the community, no amount of public relations will avail."[24] Now the United States Chamber of Commerce, by establishing "Nation's Business," and the National Association of Manufacturers, through a widespread public relations program to explain business to the public, were ready to accept true public relations as an integral part of the business picture. And now, U. S. Steel, A. T. & T., General Motors, Standard Oil of New Jersey, along with hundreds of other major industries, through campaigns that attempted to integrate business life into the life and thinking of the people, were ready to accept public relations counsel on the terms stated by H. J. Pringle in the *American Mercury;* ". . . the first task of the public relations counsel . . . is to see (that) his client offers something which the public can be brought to accept."[25] Since the American public was now growing up, learning about business, and willing to accept only what it felt was in its best interests, American industry "had now become an individual enterprise devoted to public business."[26]

So, too, by 1940, had public relations as an art and as a profession grown up. Truly, it had now reached Eric Goldman's "Two-Way Street." Scores

---

[24]In an address to the Association of National Advertisers
[25]*Mass Psychologist*—Feb. 1930
[26]Bernays—p. 106

of colleges and universities were offering a wide selection of courses on public relations. Recognition as a profession of its own was granted by the advertising business, by encyclopedias and dictionaries, by industry, and, best of all, by most of its own practitioners. Public relations now contained only one real failing, a drawback that remains to this day: it is almost impossible to evaluate directly the effectiveness of a public relations program. It is part of the overall activities of any good business. Yet its results cannot be counted in dollars and cents. Public relations today remains a form of social statesmanship embodying ". . . a field of theory and practice dealing with the relationships of people to the society on which they are dependent for their maintenance and growth."[27]

Unique Society of Free Men

Yet there is still some hesitancy and ambivalence in defining its true nature. In 1958, the *Encyclopedia Americana*, using over four and one-half pages to discuss Public Relations, still said that there is ". . . little agreement on its precise definition, its proper scope, or its practical responsibilities."[28]

Despite this, there is, today, almost universal recognition of the public relations counsel, his profession, and of the place he holds in today's business environment. As well as by anyone, it was stated by President Conant of Harvard in 1948: "As never before, business needs men who appreciate the responsibilities of business to itself and to that unique society of free men which has been developed on this continent. Such men must understand not only the practical workings of business organizations, but also the economic and social climate in which business operates: they must be as well trained as our professional men in law and medicine."[29]

[27] *Ibid.*—p. 122
[28] P. 768
[29] *The Responsibilities of Business Leadership*—Harvard University Press

SYB

ADMINISTRATIVE PUBLIC RELATIONS

For too long, an aura of mysticism has enveloped the concepts of public relations. The area has become so confused that if the leading professional public relations men in the country were brought together in one room, they probably would not be able to arrive at a satisfactory definition of the subject. I say this despite the fact that there have been many attempts to define public relations:

> PUBLIC RELATIONS, the activities connected with interpreting and improving the relationships of an organization or an individual with the public . . . those (public relations men) who operate on a policy making level, so that they have a voice not only in securing publicity for the activities of their employers, but also in making those activities conform to the public interest.
>
> The basic purpose of a public relations department is the establishment and maintenance of good will. It is obvious that the more the organization does to merit this good will, the easier the task of the public relations director will be . . .

Encyclopaedia Britannica

The efficient public relations executive, therefore, works forcefully for the elimination of policies that he believes to be open to criticism.

Funk & Wagnalls New Practical Standard Dictionary of the English Language

PUBLIC RELATIONS. Those functions of an enterprise, organization, army, etc., that acquaint the general public with its activities, purposes and accomplishments.

Webster's New Collegiate Dictionary

PUBLIC RELATIONS. The activities of a corporation, union, government, or other organization in building and maintaining sound and productive relations with special publics such as customers, employees, or stockholders, and with the public at large, so as to adapt itself to its environment and interpret itself to society.

It is evident that the layman who studies these definitions will gain little real understanding of the scope and functions of public relations, other than these abstract thoughts: "... making those activities conform to the public interest," ". . . establishment and maintenance of good will," ". . . acquaint the general public," ". . . interpret itself to society."

This book has been written to give YOU a better understanding of public relations, with particular emphasis on my theory of Administrative Public Relations.

Administrative public relations combines the best of management consulting procedures with a working knowledge of public relations. It accepts and applies psychological and sociological techniques. It utilizes all established methods of publicity. It understands the tried and true value of "Ballyhoo." It makes use of every principle of creativity. And, it applies all of these practices on an individual basis to fit the specific needs of any problem.

My theory of Administrative Public Relations, then, is an extension of public relations as it is normally practiced—a sophistication.

With skill, time and money, it is possible to develop and project any image. Living up to that image, however, is a lot more difficult. This is where Administrative Public Relations differs from established practices.

True administrative public relations is only a reflection of what you really are.

It is my belief that it is necessary to begin to mold an image **internally**. Administrative Public Relations is not concerned with what actions **look** best to the public; it is only concerned that the projected image be **true**.

In the trick mirrors of a carnival fun house, it is possible to see an elongated reflection, a diminished reflection or a true reflection, depending on which mirror is looked into. However, it is always obvious which mirrors present the distorted images.

In-Depth Study

The public has a mental image of the services or products that you present. If you don't live up to that image it is not a true one, and the public's respect can instantly be shattered. For a professional man, this image can be shattered when a patient or client steps into his office; for the businessman the moment a customer enters his store; or for the city the instant a visitor enters.

You can reflect only what you truly are.

When I accept a client, I begin by making an in-depth study of his internal organization. This does not mean getting a quick, surface picture of the field. It requires a concentrated, extensive research job; learning all the practices, all the ethical, historical and emotional factors involved. Only when I am aware of every facet of the operation can I make positive recommendations. Obviously, to produce long-lasting, effective results in a public relations program, a professional public relations consultant cannot come in "off the street" with a complete campaign.

A thorough understanding of the operation and its relationship to the community is necessary before presenting an image to the public.

Those of you who, after reading this book, will develop your own public relations programs, are in an advantageous position: no one is as well aware of the internal structure of your operation as you are.

To begin your program of Administrative Public Relations, examine these four areas as they apply to you:

1. Attitude: Your attitude and reaction to the people with whom you deal is of prime importance. How far will you extend yourself in "special services" for these people? If you are a businessman who offers a warranty on a product, do you cheerfully stand behind that warranty?

2. Initial Contact: Examine the first impression a visitor has when entering your establishment. Does the visitor's initial opinion of you concur with the image that you are trying to project? If you are a modern physician, does your office provide an up-to-date professional appearance?

3. Communications: Once the visitor has entered your establishment you must be able to project your entire image and philosophy. Do you develop a rapport between the visitor and your operation? If you are a politician, campaigning for public office, are you able to get across to the voter your personality, ideas and programs?

Do You Keep in Touch?

4. Continuing Relationships: After establishing initial contact and communications, you must be able to maintain a continuing relationship. Do you keep in touch with the visitor once he has left your establishment? If you are an association, do you continually keep your members informed of your activities?

Once these four principal areas of concern have been analyzed, keeping in mind the information on the operation, a comprehensive Administrative Public Relations program can be planned.

In the following chapters I have tried to avoid

the trap into which many other books in this field fall. There are no glittering generalities; no vague, intangible concepts.

You will find a simple, practical, step-by-step guide which will lead you to the successful development of your own Administrative Public Relations program—so that you can **sell yourself big.**

BUSINESSMEN

Advertising and public relations are two distinctly different modes of communication. Each is an entity in itself. Each serves a different purpose. One is "tune," the other "lyrics." While the two make beautiful music together, one cannot replace the other.

This fundamental principle especially applies to the businessman. Public relations cannot be substituted for advertising.

What public relations can do is make the businessman's advertising dollar stretch farther. It supplements his advertising efforts. It gets the businessman news coverage through legitimate communication channels. It helps set the proper image, through which his public relations and his advertising project a consistent reflection of his operation.

In building his image, the major problem that confronts the businessman is precisely what type of reflection he wants to project.

The decision as to what image the businessman should be presenting must, of necessity, be left entirely up to him as a merchandiser.

However, the decision can be based on several concrete factors: 1. the type of merchandise carried; 2. the type of socio-economic area in which the business is located; 3. the businessman's previous job experience; and 4. the personality of the businessman.

After selecting an image, the next question becomes, will the businessman have the determination to stay with it?

The Worried Merchant

It is quite possible that the businessman may become concerned over the immediate success and acceptance of the image he is trying to build. If he becomes uncertain over his choice of image, he may try to change his pattern and become all things to all people.

A merchant, for example, enters the ladies clothing business and decides to cater to a finer, more sophisticated clientele. He carries a high-priced, high-styled line of apparel. But he soon discovers that the neighborhood women are interested in his store only to come in and browse, then leave without buying.

The merchant becomes a bit uneasy, wondering if there is enough trade among the higher income group in his area to warrant his continuing high-priced operation. He may think that by bringing in a line of moderately priced dresses to supplement his stock he will increase the number of potential customers in his area.

When this doesn't improve matters, our worried merchant may next decide to put in a low-priced, bargain line, hoping that he will now have universal price appeal for all women entering his store. The result, is that he satisfies no one. He has spread himself too thin and has destroyed any semblance of the image he started out to create.

Two Prime Choices

In this day of the department store, the discount house and the food store chain—the small businessman is left with two prime choices if he is to survive against this overpowering competition that surrounds him: he must either grow and become a "big" businessman or he must become a specialty shop, offering a select line of merchandise, good personal service and close customer relations.

Because of the large capital investment needed for the small business to grow big, this course is limited to very few. If the small businessman selects the second course of action—the specialty shop—maintaining the image of the specialty line becomes all-important. There's the story, set in the depression era, of the poor immigrant who could neither read nor write but who had an inborn genius for cooking and serving food at its finest. Of course, he opened a restaurant.

Despite the depression, his restaurant flourished. So much so that it became the showplace of the city. So much so that he could afford to send his son to the most expensive university to specialize in business administration.

While the son was gone, the restaurant became more successful, more lavish and more popular. The restaurateur had built an image.

When the son returned, armed with his degree, he set out to show his father how a business should be run, took one look at the elaborate operation and threw up his hands in horror.

"What are you doing?" he asked his bewildered father, "Don't you know we're in the midst of a depression? The key phrase today is 'economy through efficiency'."

True to his teaching, the son immediately began to effect economies. He fired half the help which had made the restaurant's service so good. He had billboards taken down, newspaper advertising budget cut to the bone, menus mimeographed instead of printed in full color.

And So Business Sagged

With each act of "efficiency" business sagged—and with each drop in business the son initiated another economy measure. Soon the inevitable occurred. The restaurateur went bankrupt.

When questioned about his misfortune, the immigrant had only this to say, "One thing I am grateful for. I was able to send my son to college and if it were not for *his* education I never would have learned we were in a depression."

A good example of the principle that once a businessman has set a particular image he should stay with it.

The question now becomes: How does a business establish an image?

Many elements go into building a public picture of a businessman. As I have mentioned, the price structure of his product, the quality of his merchandise, his service and the area in which he is located begin the picture; from there the businessman adds the deft brush strokes that must enhance that portrait.

Logotype of an Image

One of the first things the businessman should do is develop a logotype—a symbol that represents him, his type of business and his mode of operation. A logotype should be a trademark which becomes associated with that businessman, and which is immediately identifiable in the public's mind. This logotype, or logo, should then be used on every type of printed matter that is offered for public attention. It should be used on his stationery and invoices, his newspaper ads, his boxes and wrapping paper, his store sign, and any other material that will be seen by the public.

The development of the proper logo, one that best symbolizes the firm or business, is a highly creative act. Capturing precise imagery is a problem of intangible proportions. "Giants" of industry spend hundreds of thousands of dollars to hire creative talents who develop their corporate symbols.

I can't ask the small businessman to do this. But there is always the local art studio or artist, who, given the problem, can submit various sketches that convey the proper "feel."

Another phase of the businessman's over-all public relations program is personal exposure. He must get out and meet the public. He cannot sit in his store and wait for the public to come to him.

Well designed logos or symbols have an important function in a business. They should be used on all stationery, business cards and promotional materials, so that the customer comes to identify the symbol with the business. Logos should be professionally designed to depict the nature of the business.

As in the case of the professional man, the businessman must be a "joiner" and a "leader." He must be known; make his presence felt through his participation in community affairs.

These activities get the businessman legitimate news coverage in the local magazines and news media. His name in print, coinciding with his advertising, helps to build community identity.

If the businessman is an officer in a civic group, he can utilize his position to suggest that meetings be held in his place of business. By doing this he is performing a public service. At the same time he draws attention to his position in the business community and attracts new clients.

Adding the Personal Touch

By adding a "personal touch," such as serving coffee and rolls to his guests, he conveys the warm and friendly atmosphere of his establishment.

In guiding the small businessman toward the processing of his own public relations program, I must stress that he be imaginative and receptive to new ideas. There is no greater reason for change, no better time for change, than when the businessman feels that this is ". . . the tried and true method" . . . or that "the business has been doing it this way for the past 50 years." When this occurs, the time is ripe for change. Just because the store has sent out the same form letter since 1932, or has had the same July Clearance Sale since grandfather founded the place, is no reason, in itself, to continue the practice. The businessman who is progressive, who discards old ideas, who tries new and sometimes radical things, is the one who eventually will make the most profound impression on the community.

Off-season ideas and promotions may be refreshing, may be much more apt to create interest, buyer enthusiasm and response. Different methods of communication, particularly by mail because of the relatively low cost, are certain to receive greater attention.

Avoid the Circular File

For example, rather than the routine, conventional flyer, I advocate the use of the personal letter. The flyer, even if it is extremely well done and is particularly attractive or promotes a product which has immediate consumer demand, is quite likely to get the usual third class treatment—a toss into the "circular file."

A first-class mailed letter, personally written and addressed, is going to attain a higher rate of interest and readership. It is certainly a more expensive method, but if there is a budget problem I suggest that mailings be made less frequently, or perhaps your mailing list can be reduced selectively to cut down the cost.

Secretarial services are available and automatic typewriter systems in use by which many letters are actually typed at one time and the personal salutation is typed into position at a later time. At this writing, the cost of this service in my area is approximately 18 cents each.

CENTRAL 6-3800

ALSO IN DETROIT

WABASH AT MADISON

CHICAGO 2, ILLINOIS

February 21, 1966

Dear Mr.

Our selection of GRAHAM & GUNN clothes for spring is more extensive than we have previously offered. We introduced these clothes last year, and it has been most gratifying to have many of our customers express their pleasure in wearing them.

One of the most outstanding and attractive suitings for spring-into-summer wear is a blend of Dacron polyester, wool and mohair in a very subtle stripe. The fabric is amazingly wrinkle-resistant and luxurious to wear.

After examining the enclosed swatch, we believe you will agree that this GRAHAM & GUNN suit, priced at $110, is designed and executed in the manner of our finest clothes.

We look forward to showing you our GRAHAM & GUNN collection.

Cordially yours,

George Campbell

FINE MENS WEAR

A well-written personal sales letter to a customer from a salesman, giving information on new merchandise, is an excellent public relations vehicle.

The personal letter becomes an advertising medium integrated with your public relations program that proves to be an effective means of communication, because you have now added a personal touch. You are developing a warm approach to your clients or customers by communicating feelings of interest and friendship.

Appealing to Mrs. Jones

Speaking of warmth and friendship, if this is the image you wish to project, this attitude should reach beyond the personal letter and into the place-of-business itself.

The importance of a cordial, casual atmosphere cannot be over-emphasized. It is one of the advantages that the specialty shop has over the huge, impersonal department store or discount house.

The giant retail business operations can offer one-stop shopping, a wide variety within a particular department, delivery service, monthly budgeting and lower prices. But one detracting element the giant stores cannot avoid is impersonality—and this is something of great importance to the customer.

How appealing it is to Mrs. Jones to be able to walk into her favorite neighborhood store and be greeted with a warm, "Hello, Mrs. Jones. How did Debbie like that party dress you bought her?"

How important it is to her to be able to come into a store and merely browse, ask price, "try something on" with no thought of buying at that time. Perhaps she just wants a chance to get out of her house and chat with you for a few moments. When the time comes to buy—she'll buy at your store.

This is the kind of image you can establish that no department store can duplicate.

Service With a Smile

Should you employ several people in your establishment, get them into the habit of remembering names. And, get them to impress *their* names on the customer's mind. This can be done by using name tags, or through a: "Thanks for your purchase. Next time you come in, why don't you ask for me. My name is Sally." This creates a personal tie. Also, returning to the personalized direct-mail program, letters written to the customer may now be signed by the sales person who is familiar to that customer.

Many retail slogans have been developed through the years, some by the nation's historically prominent business leaders: "Service with a smile," "the customer is always right," "satisfaction guaranteed or your money back." Although these slogans have become part of the business jargon, many of them are given only lip service; yet all of them are image builders which have greater significance today than they did when they originally were coined. They are business philosophies that should be unalterable and, once established, avidly adhered to.

Take the case of the money back guarantee, for example. If, in keeping with your image of casual, warm, no-high-pressure shopping you establish a policy of money back guarantee—practice that policy liberally and *with a smile*.

The Importance of Attitude

The Myron Cohen story comes to mind, in which two friendly retailers met on the street. After chatting a while, Mr. Goldfarb said, "Sam, why don't you ask me how's business?"

"All right, Jake, so how is business?"

"Don't ask!" came the troubled reply. "Monday, all day long, I sold just one suit. Tuesday I didn't make one sale. And Wednesday was even worse than Tuesday."

Sam looked bewildered. "What do you mean? If you didn't sell anything Tuesday, how could Wednesday be worse than Tuesday?"

"Well, Wednesday," Jake explained, "the man who bought the suit Monday brought it back."

No retailer likes to lose a sale. He likes less to make a sale only to have the merchandise returned. Fortunately, the "professional returner," one type of shopper that plagues every store, is in the minority. Most shoppers are embarrassed to return items sold to them in good faith. Still, making it easy for the customer to return an item, makes it easier for him to buy another.

It is up to the shop owner to make his customer feel perfectly at ease. Accept the return graciously and you make not only a friend, but also a better customer and an invaluable medium for word-of-mouth advertising. This, then, becomes part of your image. The manner in which you accept such returns can help make or break that image.

This returned-merchandise policy is more of a public relations "attitude" for the small businessman, than it is a strict public relations practice. Which brings us to another bit of general advice for the small businessman directing his own public relations program—the importance of attitude.

In my concept of Administrative Public Relations, the word "attitude" takes on a much broader meaning than just the "feeling" or "mood" of a given situation.

The first function of the businessman is to define and understand his own attitude. The businessman is attempting to make the public aware of his well-delineated image. He must be just as aware of that image himself, and his attitude should reflect it. For example, he cannot promote a personalized business and then have his sales people forget or ignore the names of his regular customers. As I discussed previously, Administrative Public Relations begins at home. Before you present a public relations program to the people, your "home" must be prepared with the proper merchandise, facilities and personnel that enhance your image. Remember, your attitude toward, and understanding of, your own image is the key to a successful public relations program.

Know Your Customers

The second function of the businessman's "attitude" must be directed toward his customers. After you get over the initial drive and excitement of conceiving your own public relations program, lock yourself in your office, sit back in your chair, and consider for a few moments how **you** would receive this public relations program if **you** were a customer instead of a businessman. Consider what your customer's attitude is likely to be toward your business. Consider how your new public relations program will fit into this image. If you are attempting to change an old, undesirable image, consider whether it should be done quickly, or in a subtle, gradual way. If you are designing a logo, show the artist's sketch of it to a few of your customers to see how they like it before you make your final decision. If you are considering putting in a different line of merchandise, talk to a few friends and customers whom you know have good taste before you make the change. But, be careful. Remember that because your friends and customers have a preconceived idea of your business's past image, they may not be overly receptive to change. This, too, may be an indication of the direction you will have to take.

Straying from the Tried and True

Your attitude, or awareness of your customer, will also be of great aid to you in a more concrete form. Be sure you know who your customers are! Here I am not talking about their names or faces, but generally, of age and income level, number of children, type of cars they drive, type of homes they live in, their religions and hobbies, the civic organizations they belong to, businesses they are in, and the type of neighborhoods in which they live. Know what their problems are, and where their interests lie. If your average customer is a woman, in her thirties, with three young children, in a middle income neighborhood, owns one car which her husband drives to work every day, it may be difficult for her to leave her home. Therefore, it may pay to provide some sort of a delivery service or telephone ordering service for her convenience.

I mentioned previously that one of the most important avenues toward building a distinctive personality for the small businessman and his opera-

Beverly is working nights...
for your convenience

BEVERLY DODGE, that is . . . with the finest auto-servicing facilities on the south side, now goes one step further. Starting March 1st . . .

SERVICE DEPARTMENT
OPEN 'TIL 9 P.M.
MONDAY THRU FRIDAY

No problems trying to get your car to us during the working day. Same fast service . . . same reasonable charges.

Call our Service Manager, Vern Stull, to set up a date (night service by appointment only).

And, whether it's service, a new Dodge, or a fine, budget-priced used car, be sure to see Beverly.

1500 WEST 95th STREET
PHONE 239-4900

Arrange to have your business open on odd days or hours to increase the shopping convenience of those who may be working or tied up during the normal course of a business day.

tion is imagination and reception to new ideas. This was related in terms of writing personalized letters, and of avoiding routine and set patterns.

There are many other ways in which new ideas can be incorporated into a business. For example, in the case of a retail business, why not try changing your normal evening hours? If the idea meets with the approval of the local chamber of commerce and does not infringe on any blue laws or religious restrictions, why not a family market day on Sunday? This could be promoted as a special event, developed to permit the entire family to participate in a shopping outing. Promotion and advertising of the event could take almost any form: direct mail, radio, TV, newspapers, local magazines, posters and window displays. The idea is particularly applicable to businesses concerned with "big" purchases, such as furniture stores, TV and appliance stores, automobile dealerships—any area in which "big ticket" purchasing may concern the entire family.

Another sample of straying from the "tried and true" routine: Why not, in the case of a ladies apparel shop, have a "men's night only" at Christmas time? Close the store entirely to women for the night and permit men to shop for gifts for their wives. Serve coffee and have models display the latest in fashions, and the man will actually *enjoy* his shopping excursion. He will then have time to shop at ease, without embarrassment, and he will mark *this* store as the place to buy all of his wife's gifts.

The same situation, of course, can be reversed. That is, a men's store can promote a "lady's night," when women can select ties, shirts or accessories without catching the male shopper at the end of the counter grimacing at her taste in men's accessories.

One Hand Washes the Other

Still another example of procedural innovation is the reciprocal arrangement: combining the public relations efforts of two stores whose operations complement each other. Two stores can, by verbal suggestion, store signs and direct mailings, promote each other through their separate customers. This one-hand-washes-the-other arrangement can be entered into by many related operations, such as: the travel agency and the luggage shop, the sports store and the men's sportswear shop, the book store and children's apparel store, or the men's store and the women's clothing store.

A specific example: One of my clients was a ladies' apparel shop, in business a relatively short time and contemplating a grand opening sale. I knew that the owner of this shop was friendly with the proprietor of a men's store that catered to the same class of trade. The owner of the men's shop was approached and asked for permission to use his mailing list. He was surprised at the request, particularly since I informed him that our letter would be addressed to the men. After I explained our cooperative public relations idea, he agreed to participate because he saw that his own store could gain a great deal from the promotion.

Constant Double Exposure

The letter took the approach that since the man was a discriminating buyer, as evidenced by his patronage of this men's store, he probably would be interested in knowing that a ladies' apparel shop of equivalent stature was having a grand opening sale. Now he would have the opportunity to purchase gifts of discrimination for his wife and, perhaps, the next time he visited this very fine men's store he might wish to have his wife join him so that they could shop together at both places.

This particular letter had a two-fold purpose. While it promoted the men's shop and appealed to the husband, it very effectively performed the function of announcing and advertising the ladies' store —to a known buyer. Even though it was addressed to the personal attention of the husband, we were certain that the great majority of these letters would be read first by the wife!

This initial reciprocal arrangement worked out so well that the two stores now have a permanent working agreement which lends itself to constant double exposure—double promotion at no additional cost.

I have cited only a few examples of how the businessman can be different; how his image can be fresh and novel. Many more could be described. Other public relations activities present themselves as situations and circumstances arise that are particularly pertinent to a specific merchant, or unique to his locale. This is an attempt to stimulate him, and you, into thinking in this more imaginative vein and to alert you to the opportunities that present themselves for good public imagery—imagery that contributes to the success of your operation.

The Chamber of Commerce

To this point, I have discussed the businessman and how he can present the proper reflection of his own image. A key facet of "image presentation" for the businessman is the role he can and should play in his local chamber of commerce. Acting as a part of a larger organization, the businessman's activities can greatly affect his own business, through the chamber of commerce, for the good of the entire community.

It is superfluous to say that one businessman at times can remain aloof from the entire business community in any town or city. In some areas he can operate independently, making his own merchandising and marketing decisions. However, there are many areas where he cannot operate efficiently as an individual.

No businessman can create the proper image of himself when the area in which he is located and the neighbors who surround him do not lend themselves to that image.

A man may rationalize his failure to support the local chamber of commerce by maintaining that it is not as progressive as it should be, or that it does not reflect his personal business philosophies, or that it does nothing to promote his business.

All I can say in this case is that the chamber, though a national organization, is organized locally; and if it is failing in any way, it is not the concept of the chamber, but the fault of the local membership.

The chamber of commerce should play a vital role in stimulating the growth and prosperity of the community. It has much to contribute, and the businessman has much to gain by participating in its activities. But, like the individual businessman, the chamber can restrict itself to routine, or it can seek fresh, creative thinking—explore and implement the novel and the exciting. The individual businessman is affected by the course of action his chamber takes, even if he is not a member.

Aimed at One Goal

The several functions of the chamber of commerce are aimed at one goal: stimulating business within its scope of influence. As the chamber works toward this goal, it promotes business for the entire area and increases the revenue of individual members. The more each member does to aid the chamber in obtaining its goals, the more the individual stands to profit by his labors.

The chamber must wield political influence. To some, "political influence" becomes a questionable phrase; it seems fraught with corruption or double-dealing. This is not what's meant.

Political influence, in this case, is the *active opposition* to those in government or those running for office whose expressed opinions or actions are harmful to the community and the *active support* of those whose platforms are beneficial to the area.

Political influence also plays a vital role in community business life. Obviously, many political decisions, on the local, state and national levels, affect the business community. In a political situation of this sort, a large national corporation has the money and the personnel to make its opinions felt. An individual businessman cannot voice an effective opinion by himself; but by grouping together in a chamber of commerce, a small businessman *can* get a hearing from government officials. A representative of a local chamber can be heard at a city council meeting, and his views are listened to and respected because he represents an organized group of individual businessmen with the combined dollars and community to warrant attention.

Too often a chamber of commerce takes the position that it is solely a "business group," and that it must remain non-political.

I maintain that because this *is* a business group, it must be a political group as well. So much can be done to enhance the business district, to attract traffic, to provide added conveniences for the shopper; things that can be accomplished only through political activities by a chamber of commerce.

Financial support should be provided by the chamber to help stimulate and develop progressive and far-sighted programs for the community. It must work closely with the political, civic and social organizations that also operate in the community. And, it must help to provide the manpower.

Further, the chamber should be directly concerned with the cleanliness and appearance of the community. It must campaign for and help stimulate the remodeling of aging store fronts, should help rent empty stores that give the area a downgraded atmosphere; should entice new business into the area; and should help the area preserve the image of a fresh and thriving community.

The Basic Problem Areas

Working to obtain a favorable political climate and a progressive community, the chamber should determine whether it has done everything within its power to make the area conducive for shopping. Is there enough police protection to assure safe and relaxed night shopping? Is traffic congestion kept to a minimum? Has the parking problem been alleviated in the best, most practical manner? These are some of the basic problem areas in which the chamber of commerce functions.

Now let's move beyond general chamber of commerce goals. Let's approach public relations for the chamber, much as we did for the individual merchant. Let us seek new, unusual, fresh avenues by which we can build a "climate of awareness" and create an aura of excitement, progressiveness and consumer interest.

In considering public relations at the chamber of commerce level, let me become specific, detailing a few actual promotions which I have successfully employed to stimulate business.

I previously discussed the deviation from routine store opening hours by the individual merchant. The same can be done by an entire shopping area.

On a Warm Summer Evening

Let us select a warm summer evening and, instead of the usual store hours, let's consider promoting a "Midnight Fiesta." All stores announce that they will be open from 10 p.m. to 1 a.m.

Now we create a festive atmosphere in keeping with a "Midnight Fiesta."

The entire area is decorated for the occasion. Lampposts, store fronts, hanging banners—everything is designed to emphasize the Spanish theme of the event.

Posters are placed in store windows announcing the event, and press releases are submitted to all local newspapers and radio stations. Store interiors are decorated accordingly.

After the late store hours are over a party is held. A center is selected where, at a given hour, all will congregate for entertainment, refreshments and dancing. Tickets of admission to the party are distributed free by participating merchants to customers. During the shopping hours Mariachi bands stroll the streets.

Community and youth organizations can be called upon to participate, by helping to provide entertainment and refreshments. In keeping with the fiesta theme, the chamber can sponsor a parade.

High school bands can be used and local industry can be asked to provide floats or displays.

There are no limits to the embellishments that can be added to this basic idea. It depends only on how elaborate the chamber wishes to make the event. Balloons can be imprinted for the children; there can be a fireworks display for the teenagers; a beauty contest; search lights and pan lights to focus attention to the area.

By promotion and careful attention to details, the evening becomes a family shopping and entertainment event. This type of promotion is talked about for weeks prior to, and after, the event. Attendance is excellent. The business district gets immeasurably valuable publicity, public attention and increased business volume.

Conversation Piece

Obviously, an event of this type must be carefully planned. All details must be spelled out and a schedule programmed. Committees must be appointed to handle separate areas of the event, and one man must be placed in charge of the project to oversee all the details. Budgets for each separate area must be assigned. The organization, financing and execution of an event of this type is within the scope of almost every chamber of commerce.

Another chamber of commerce public relations event with which I have had a great deal of success is a "Gift Wrapping Center" during the Christmas shopping season.

During the height of the Christmas season it is not unusual to find that a small store does not have the time or the personnel to provide an adequate gift wrapping service. Department stores can set up gift wrapping sections, but they charge customers for this service.

This is where the chamber of commerce steps in. Each member contributes a specified sum to cover the cost of promotion and implementation of the service. An empty store in a convenient location is selected and personnel, experienced in gift wrapping, are employed. Banners in the stores of participating merchants announce the "Gift Wrapping Center" program. Newspaper ads are purchased to further inform the community. A Santa Claus can pass out handbills.

All shoppers purchasing items in a chamber of commerce store get tickets permitting them to bring the merchandise to the center for free gift wrapping. While they are waiting for their packages to be wrapped, coffee can be served; the "Gift Wrapping Center" can be decorated with signs or displays from cooperating shops. This gives the customer a chance to consider other Christmas purchases while he waits for his package.

It Takes a Little Vision

In this program, I have discovered that the average cost per gift wrapping is 20 cents. I have learned that the customer appreciates the convenience of a wrapping service so much that he'd gladly pay more. The center gives participating merchants a competitive advantage over non-cooperating stores. It increases sales volume for the shopping district and enhances the community's business image.

The two promotions we have described go far beyond the normal semi-annual chamber of commerce clearance sales and the annual Christmas decorations for the shopping district streets. They are different, creative, interesting, and they stimulate business. More and more chambers are beginning to look this way for aggressive and progressive sales-stimulating activities. The two-day art fair and the plaza party are becoming more popular.

Always be on the lookout for community or seasonal events which may lend themselves to shopping promotions. All it takes is a little vision, a bit of creativity and enthusiasm, and some concerted effort. It pays! Here is an excellent opportunity for a chamber of commerce to sell itself and to help you SELL YOURSELF BIG.

PROFESSIONAL MEN

Public relations is reflected in every thought, deed and action of the professional man. Every time he shakes a patient's hand, writes a client a letter, makes a significant comment at a community or fraternal meeting, chooses the proper decor for his waiting room, even picks the right tie to go with his suit, he reflects his image.

Physicians, dentists, attorneys, accountants and other professional men are prohibited by ethical practices from using some avenues of communication such as advertising, that are open to the businessman or firm. How simple it would be for the professional man to get exposure if he could resort to the billboard or the TV commercial. The surgeon would get public notice if he could advertise "cheapest appendectomies in town," or a dentist with a special 2-for-1 sale on extractions.

I am not attempting in this chapter to discuss academically the ethics, morals and codes of conduct of professional men; or things that should or should not be done in the public interest. I will be concerned only with giving the professional man some of the techniques of Administrative Public Relations that can help him enhance his public image, keeping in mind that nothing discussed here will violate any professional ethics or codes.

Since the professional man usually cannot make use of the normal means of advertising, he must seek other methods of exposing his professional capabilities to the community. His most powerful tool is public relations.

Problems confronting the professional man in gaining public awareness and acceptance include the initial establishment of his practice, and the stimulation and growth of that practice, once the foundation has been laid.

Let us examine the first problem. Unlike the businessman who advertises a store's opening in newspapers and by mail, the professional man cannot promote a "grand opening."

He Becomes the Spearhead

He must introduce his services to his community in another way. The key word here is "introduce." In order to "introduce" himself to the community, the professional man should join social, civic and fraternal organizations. He should contribute his time, his ideas and his efforts to these organizations. He doesn't join more organizations than he can handle, for he must do a creditable job in each. Through these activities he makes his neighbors aware of his existence. More than that, he can now begin to convince his community that he is *personally* competent.

He strives to become a "thought leader" in the community. *He* becomes the one who proposes the plan to save money on Main Street's Christmas decorations. He becomes the one who spearheads the community conservation effort. He becomes the one who chairs this year's community fund drive.

The community becomes aware of his leadership ability, reliability and personal competence.

The layman cannot judge the doctor, lawyer or accountant on the basis of professional competence. He cannot, for example, weigh the professional skills and judgment of one physician against another.

Gaining confidence and respect for the professional man's performance in community life, the layman is most apt to transfer these impressions and use them as a basis to judge professional capabilities.

As the professional man's name becomes linked with his contributions to community projects, his efforts in behalf of civic and fraternal activities become newsworthy enough to be given editorial coverage in the local newspapers. He now becomes known not only to his club's co-workers, but also to the general public.

His public relations work has begun.

Wife's Value to Practice

One cannot do justice to a discussion of public relations for the professional man, without mentioning his wife. Her knowledge of the practice and her interest in its success are of tremendous importance.

Because the professional man is necessarily tied to the office during working hours, his wife should become his daytime representative to the community. She can help build the practice by her active participation in civic life. Her value to the practice in making new friends and neighbors is incalculable.

The PTA offers excellent opportunities for the wife. The wife of a health practitioner can make mothers and teachers aware of the need for periodic examinations, and she can underscore the relationship of good health to proper school achievement.

The wife of the lawyer or accountant can be influential in civic activities such as community councils and the League of Women Voters.

Auxiliary Newsworthy

Bond issues, school taxes and local referendums are all matters upon which some professional men can speak judiciously. The wife, working within a civic organization, can create the atmosphere which opens the door for an invitation to the professional man to speak about these matters.

The professional wife is limited by the same restrictions that limit the professional man in joining organizations. She should not take on more than she can handle successfully. No worse image is created than in joining an organization and then not participating in its activities.

Because of the part the wife can play in the success of a practice, it is important that she be able to discuss basic questions pertaining to that practice.

However, she should avoid the danger of making statements beyond basic concepts of her layman's knowledge of the practice. She should not cast herself in the role of the professional.

Don't overlook the importance that her participation in the ladies auxiliary to the professional association can play in the total public relations of the practice. Projects that she participates in as an auxiliary member are much more likely to be reported in local media than are the actions of the professional man. Auxiliary projects, because they usually combine a worthwhile cause with a social activity, are always covered in the women's pages of newspapers and local magazines. Here is a way for the professional man to get his name to the public, without compromising professional ethics—through his wife's activities.

The professional has begun to build an image of reliability, leadership and competence. Soon his new friends, new neighbors, the people who have read about him, will be coming to see him on a "professional" basis.

He now faces the critical challenge of maintaining the personal image he established in the community, as he projects it at the *professional* level.

And remember, the image that the patient or client has of the professional, can be shattered the moment he sets foot into the professional's office.

Old Magazines Gone?

What sort of first impression do you, as a professional man, make? Step outside the door of your inner office, into the reception room and answer these questions. Is the decor of the office in keeping with a dignified, yet modern reception area, reflecting the aura of your profession? Is the receptionist properly dressed, befitting her position? Is she well groomed? Have you thrown away your 1947 *Collier's* magazines? Have you done everything you can to make the patient or client comfortable as he waits for you?

If your answer to all these questions is a definite **"yes"**—you are most likely creating the right "first impression."

If you are not positive, let us explore some of the image builders that I like to see used in a professional office.

1. If you are in the health care field, your receptionist should be dressed in a dignified manner —in a clean, freshly pressed uniform. She should neither smoke nor chew gum while interviewing patients. As an accountant or lawyer involved in a client's intimate financial affairs, your receptionist must reflect a conservative image—one that will build confidence in you and your firm.

2. When a patient or client enters, your receptionist should immediately recognize his presence in the office, and greet him by name, if possible. She should submit to you his name and file so that you can re-acquaint yourself with his past history prior to seeing him. If, for any reason, you cannot immediately see the patient or client, your receptionist should periodically inform him that you know he is waiting and you will be with him as quickly as possible. A patient or client who waits in ignorance begins to wonder whether his relationship with you is important enough to merit your attention.

Pastels Are Cheerful

3. Your office should reflect a warm, cheery atmosphere. Psychologists tell us that color has an important relationship to man's attitudes. Pastels are cheerful; dark woods are depressing; blue and green shades transmit feelings of coolness; the reds, oranges and the yellows transmit warmth. A safe rule-of-thumb would be the use of light colored pastels.

Something else to think about is that interior decorators tell you the proper use of color will increase or decrease the impression of the size of your room.

I like to see tasteful carpeting and a vase containing fresh flowers. This always enhances the hospitality of an office. It would be wise to consult an interior decorator if you are planning a new office or redecorating your old one. If you are buying new office furniture from a large store you will find that interior decorating service often is offered by the store at no charge.

4. The patient or client visiting a professional man is usually there because of a problem. The decor of your reception area can help alleviate some of his anxieties by momentarily focusing his attention on interesting subject matter. I would suggest that you do not hang pictures in your office which relate to your profession. Old stereotyped pictures are dull and boring. How many times have you seen pictures on lawyer's walls of powder-wigged English barristers; or, in a physician's office, the pallid death bed scene. Such pictures do little to put the patient or client at ease.

Put Yourself in His Place

5. Let us now take a look at the inner office in which the patient or client is interviewed. For a moment place yourself at the opposite side of the desk and study the room from the same viewpoint that the client or patient would exercise.

Your office should reflect your professional background.

The degrees, for which you worked so hard, should be in clear view. As we stated earlier, the patient or client is not in a position to judge your professional skills. He judges your ability by the professional image you project through your actions and surroundings.

If it is necessary for the patient to move from one part of the room to another for examination purposes, consider what he sees from each position; make sure that within his field of sight there is always an object to reflect your professional image. A book shelf is almost a necessity. If your office has a professional library, the patient will assume that you are knowledgeable and that you have kept up with the latest ideas and developments in your specialty.

Look at your desk. A cluttered desk is not the sign of an overworked professional, but rather gives the appearance of a disorganized man. If you haven't the time to keep it neat, be sure your receptionist or secretary does.

6. Personal appearance is extremely important for the professional man when meeting a patient or client. Dress conservatively and in keeping with the good taste of your profession.

The lawyer or accountant may find it more convenient to work in his shirt sleeves. However, he should be sure to slip on his suit jacket and adjust his tie before meeting a client.

No matter how capable a professional you are, you will be judged to some degree on these outward appearances.

The patient or client who enters your office, does so to seek your advice and counsel.

During the time that you are performing your professional services, you will have the best opportunity to sell yourself and your profession "big."

Repay His Confidence

Be warm, understanding and cordial, but maintain your professional status. *Do not* do this, however, at the expense of "talking down" to the patient or client. As a health practitioner, discuss the phases of the examination and the purposes of your treatment. As a lawyer or an accountant, explain the law that makes it necessary to handle the case as you suggest; or why your accounting procedure is best for him. He has come to you out of respect for your professional ability. Repay that confidence by displaying respect for him and his problems.

It is not necessary to avoid the use of professional or technical terms, but be sure that you further explain them in layman's language.

Most professional associations make available, to their members, pamphlets describing the various problems that may be encountered with a patient or client.

A Feeling of Appreciation

If you are doing a good job of public relations in your office, you have been explaining these problems as you have proceeded through your examination or counseling period. However, no matter how thoroughly you have briefed your patient or client, he will only retain a small portion of the information after he leaves your office. This is the time to give him supplemental printed material prepared by your association. The patient or client now leaves your office with this material and a feeling of appreciation for your efforts in acquainting him more completely with the background of his case. Naturally, for purposes of individual identification, your name should be imprinted on these supplemental materials.

As indicated previously, administrative public relations for the professional man is reflected in his every thought, deed and action. All too often, the professional man overlooks the significant role played by such items as his stationery, the telephone manners of his receptionist, and the effectiveness of his recall system on the total image which he is attempting to project to the public.

It is important that the professional man understand that his stationery is a reflection of his taste and personality. Selected and printed in a dignified manner, it is an asset. Done without thought or planning, it can undermine all of the hard work he has put forth in developing his image. Let us examine some of the rules that the professional man should follow in the design of his stationery.

1. The first item of concern is the professional announcement card. This should be sent whenever

a practice is opened or moved to a new location, or when a new associate is taken into a practice. The discussion of the professional announcement card must be divided into two areas: a. the physical design of the card; and b. to whom cards should be sent.

Dr. Roger Smith

announces the opening of his office at

100 Professional Building

First Avenue and Center Street

Hometown, U.S.A.

By Appointment 987-6543

A neatly printed professional announcement card should be sent to clients, patients or friends when opening a new practice or moving an established one.

First Impressions Are Important

a. It is important to select a high quality paper stock for the imprinting of the card. The color should always be white or off-white. I prefer the use of a panel card of high grade, rag bond, French-fold vellum stock, preferably with a deckled edge. These announcements should be engraved. They should contain only necessary information, such as: the occasion, name of the professional man, firm name if one is involved, address, telephone number, and the effective date of the announcement. This information should be presented in the most concise form possible. Remember, this is **not** an advertisement. This is not the place to attempt to sell your services.

First impressions are important. Be sure to send these announcements via first class mail, in a stamped envelope. Do not run them through a postage meter. The envelope should be hand addressed in a neat, legible script. Typed envelopes, in this case, are too impersonal. The professional man who is limited by time or penmanship from addressing these himself, may ask his receptionist to do this, may seek the services of his wife, or may employ a professional concern which specializes in the hand addressing of announcements or invitations. These concerns can be located in the yellow pages of the local phone directory, or through companies which specialize in wedding arrangements.

b. Mailing lists for announcement cards of the professional starting in practice may be developed from the names of friends and relatives, and from the social, civic and fraternal organizations to which the professional belongs. In the case of an established practice, this list should include all present clients or patients.

2. Letterheads and envelopes should be printed on rag bond paper. The use of any colored stock other than white or off-white is not recommended. This stationery may or may not be engraved. I always prefer engraved stationery but its expense may be a prohibiting factor.

The letterhead text should be short, including only the name, address, phone number, and, in specific instances, your specialty. The professional detracts from the dignity of the stationery when the letterhead attempts to become a message in itself—noting office hours, a complete list of services, and several specialties. A physician does not list the fact that he examines the heart, liver, kidneys, and takes blood tests. However, other professional men are prone to do this within the scope of their activities.

Beware the Low-Priced Card

3. Business cards should be printed on high quality stock. I prefer the use of "thin plate." This material is smooth surfaced and pliable; it can be bent without cracking the printing, and is highly resilient.

Business cards are usually printed by one of three major processes—letterpress, offset or engraving. A fourth process in common use is that

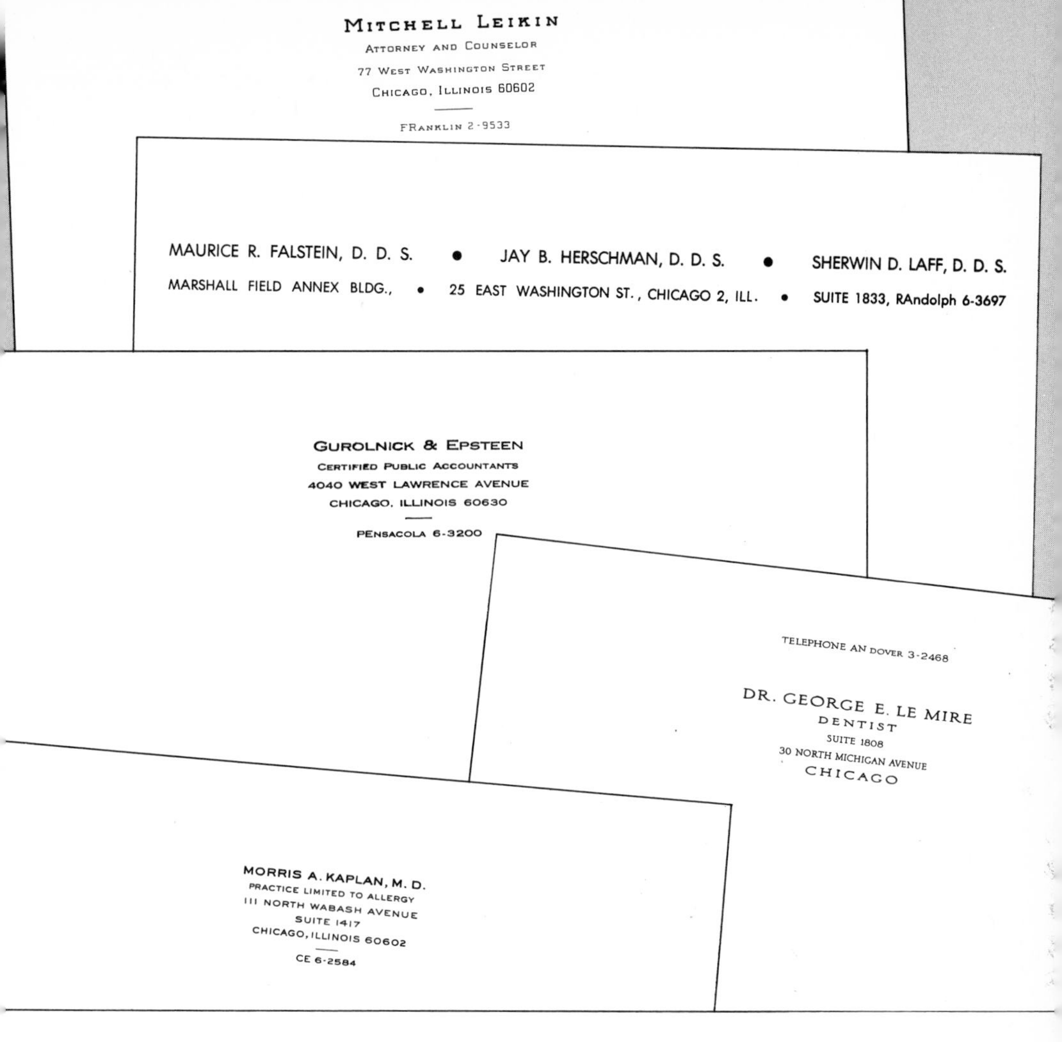

Your professional stationery is a reflection of your image. Your name, profession, specialty, address and phone number should be printed on a high quality paper stock.

of thermography, commonly referred to as "process embossed." The end result is similar in appearance to engraving; however, if this card is carried in a wallet or between other business cards, the lettering will have a tendency to smear or crack. I, therefore, do not recommend this type of printing. Also, beware of unusually low-priced cards. Cards of this type are often reproduced from rubber plate rather than cast lead type or offset plates. This is almost like printing with a rubber stamp and the result is a poor printed image.

Business cards, like your stationery, should contain no more than essential facts; name, profession, address and phone number.

Envelopes and business cards should be tastefully layed-out using a minimum of words.

4. The health care field makes wide use of the appointment card. Since I have met very few doctors who write legibly, I have developed the following rule-of-thumb. Design your appointment card so that nearly all essential information is printed. For example, rather than writing in the month and the day of the week, the months and days are printed on the card and you circle the ones which pertain to the patient's appointment.

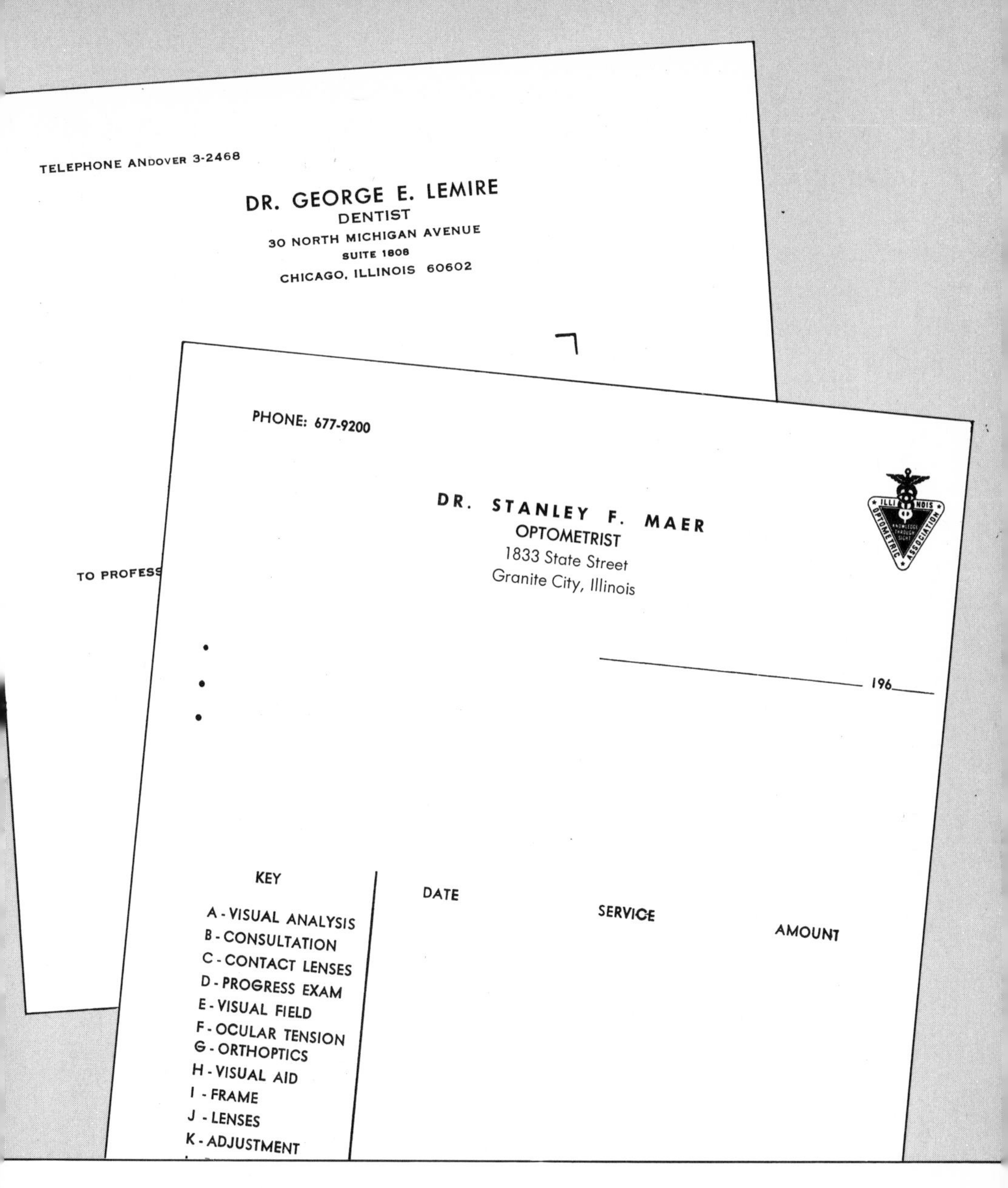

TELEPHONE ANDOVER 3-2468

DR. GEORGE E. LEMIRE
DENTIST
30 NORTH MICHIGAN AVENUE
SUITE 1808
CHICAGO, ILLINOIS 60602

TO PROFESS

PHONE: 677-9200

DR. STANLEY F. MAER
OPTOMETRIST
1833 State Street
Granite City, Illinois

196

KEY	DATE	SERVICE	AMOUNT
A - VISUAL ANALYSIS			
B - CONSULTATION			
C - CONTACT LENSES			
D - PROGRESS EXAM			
E - VISUAL FIELD			
F - OCULAR TENSION			
G - ORTHOPTICS			
H - VISUAL AID			
I - FRAME			
J - LENSES			
K - ADJUSTMENT			

Even your statement reflects your professional image. Whenever possible itemize all costs and use quality printing and paper stock.

Design the card so that you are only required to write in the date and hour.

5. Statements, like your letterheads, should be printed on high grade paper stock. I am horrified at the increasing number of professional men who send out statements which are prepared by putting the patient record through a duplicating machine. This same professional man would be the last to send out a letter on mimeograph stock, spends

The Role of Referrals

countless hours improving his office decor and professional attitudes; and yet in one moment seriously mars his professional image by the use of this highly impersonal billing method. Patients and clients seldom enjoy receiving bills; if you have been professional in your approach to now, at this delicate point, don't disturb your image.

There is a wide divergence of opinion as to whether a professional man should itemize his services. I believe that an itemized statement helps the patient or client better understand the reason for the total fee and makes him aware of the many and varied services that the professional man offers.

6. Referrals play a very important role in the professional man's life. It is because the normal avenues of advertising are closed to him that he depends to a great extent upon recommendations for the expansion of his practice. He is cognizant of this fact from the day he enters practice.

Worth Two Minutes of Time

The question arises as to how he can properly express his appreciation to those who are kind enough to refer new patients or clients to him. Some professional men use a formal imprinted "thank you" card, others fail to send any type of acknowledgement. Many of the cards are improperly done or in poor taste.

I am sure that you have seen the "thank you" card that looks like a commercial, extolling the virtues and qualifications of the professional man. The recipient of this card need not be told that you will extend to the new patient or client the same high quality, competent service that he has received in the past. If he did not sincerely believe this, he would not have made the referral initially.

Don't send a form acknowledgement or "thank you" card. It is worth two minutes of your time to write a short personal note to your patient or client expressing your appreciation for his thoughtfulness in making the referral.

These same principles apply to your relationship with other professionals who have been kind enough to refer patients or clients to you.

Another reflection upon your professional image is the action of your receptionist, secretary or nurse. And one of the principal areas of concern is the proper use of the telephone. Many patients or clients can be lost even before you have had an opportunity to meet them because of poor telephone manners.

Here are some guidelines to follow:

1. The girl who answers your telephone should have a pleasant, warm, cheerful voice. She should be bright and alert. She should communicate well with your patients or clients. Recognition of the caller's name by your girl is excellent Administrative Public Relations. A warm greeting to a client or patient familiar to your receptionist, a question by her indicating that she knows who the caller is, lets the caller know that he is remembered, and that he is important to the professional and his office staff—not just another name in the files.

2. Never permit the girl who answers your phone to inform the caller that you are too busy to talk now. The caller will understand if your girl says, "I am sorry, the doctor is with another patient. May he return your call just as soon as he is free?"

What you try to convey to the caller, in this case, is not that you are too busy to talk, but that you are engaged with someone else and are attempting to extend the same courtesies to him as you would extend to the caller if the situation were reversed.

Be Careful Screening Calls

3. If you have your receptionist screen incoming calls, be extremely cautious of the manner in which she does it. Never have her request the name of the caller first. She may then be obliged to advise him that you are out, and he may conclude that you are accepting some calls, but not his. I prefer to have a girl screen an incoming phone call by say-

ing, "Dr. Jones is out, may I please tell him who called?"

4. Your girl should be prepared to answer certain basic questions that a caller may have; and give some helpful information. Don't, however, allow your nurse to diagnose symptoms or your secretary to give legal advice.

5. If you employ a telephone answering service, you should expect it to meet the same standards that you set for your office receptionist. Because the caller might assume that he is speaking to your receptionist, the attitudes and mannerisms of the answering service personnel are as vitally important to your patient or client relationship as that of your own staff.

6. In many large cities, the telephone company offers free courses in proper telephone manners. Explore the possibilities of utilizing this service if it is available.

The professional man must develop lines of continuing communication.

This is a means of maintaining contact with the patient or client throughout the year or until professional services are again needed. It is a service which indicates that the professional is interested in the welfare of his patient or client.

Use a Newsletter

For all professional men, except attorneys, I suggest that the lines of communications be established through the use of a simplified newsletter, which ostensibly serves no other purpose than to keep the patient or client informed. No commercialism. No sell. Only pure news on such matters as new tax savings or perhaps latest developments in the health care field.

Such a service keeps the name of the professional man in front of the patient or client, and, by reporting the latest trends in his field, the professional man can open new avenues of interest for his services.

H. W. Gurolnick and Earl D. Epsteen
Certified Public Accounts
4040 WEST LAWRENCE AVENUE
CHICAGO, ILLINOIS

Highlights of 1965 Tax Law Changes

This letter is another in our series of readable digests culled from complex technical language so that our clients and friends may be better informed.

While 1964 saw a terrific income tax upheaval, 1965 has witnessed sporadic eruptions in nearly all kinds of taxes affecting the small businessman.

1. **SOCIAL SECURITY**
   a. Now has a partner called MEDICARE.
   b. New rates (including Medicare) effective January 1, 1966. Tax withholding goes from 3.625% to 4.2% . . . maximum taxable wages from $4800.00 to $6600.00.

2. **NEW VOLUNTARY SUPPLEMENTARY MEDICARE**
   A medical insurance plan
   a. For those over 65 only.
   b. Cost citizen $3.00 monthly. No cost to employer.
   c. Assists in paying doctor bills.

3. **EXCISE TAXES**
   a. All but a few eliminated as of June 22, 1965.

4. **ILLINOIS SALES TAX**
   a. New leasing tax effective August 1, 1965. Purpose: To *close the loophole* permitting equipment rentals to escape sales taxes. Same rates as sales taxes. As receipts from sales are subject to sales tax, receipts from leasing are subject to leasing tax. Important—If leasing agreement was made prior to March 1, 1965—*no tax.*
   b. New resale registration numbers for all businesses without retail registration numbers. Purposes: To require registration of all Illinois businesses: To tax all sales to non-registered Illinois purchasers. Your responsibility to yourself; require registration numbers backed up by appropriate certificates from all tax free customers. Otherwise—be prepared to pay the sales taxes yourself.
   c. An ancient State ritual has silently expired. The State sales tax investigator who visited businesses within his territory from time to time to review copies of last 3 returns is gone. Other enforcement measures such as (b) above and increased cooperation with Federal Income Tax people have taken his place. On the other hand the Federal Income Tax people now have their own territorial assigned "Investigators."

5. **INTERSTATE INCOME AND SALES TAXES**
   a. Congress has passed the "Interstate Income Law" prohibiting income tax on an out-of-state seller when the in-state activity is limited to soliciting of orders. According to tax publisher Commerce Clearing House this law "provides only doubtful guidelines." In an attempt to provide a somewhat more informative guideline for you, we have prepared a condensed analysis of the 37 states' own tax and non-tax positions on the various sales methods. This analysis is a part of this letter.
   b. Although Congress has passed no legislation with respect to state sales (use) taxes the Congressional Committee on State Taxation of Interstate Commerce made an intensive 4 year study of sales taxes—as well as State Income Taxes. It concluded that the interstate seller does indeed have a difficult time determining his State tax liability and recommends uniform legislation based on in-state business location or instate employees.
   c. There are 37 sales (use) tax states. Twenty-six (26) states (including the capital D.C.) have both income and sales taxes. Eleven (11) have income taxes only—eleven (11) have sales taxes only, and just three (3) have neither. Those three?—Indiana, Nebraska and New Hampshire, the sweepstake state.
   d. The courts lean to the states in decisions to date, but there is still a wide area of uncertainty.
   e. Our judgment—the states seem to place priority on an in-state business location such as an outlet, office, a stock of goods or other material. If this applies to you, be prepared

The professional newsletter to a client or patient is one of the best ways of establishing continuing communications.

The material necessary to prepare a professional man's newsletter can be gathered from financial newspapers, professional bulletins or journals, or can be purchased from syndicated services. The newsletter can be printed on the professional's letterhead. If syndicated services are purchased, the professional should edit the material carefully to make certain the material is applicable to his practice and his attitudes.

Unlike the health care practitioner who periodically sees his patient for regular re-examination, or the accountant who is assured of a visit from his client every tax season, the attorney, unless on retainer, sees a client only when a specific problem arises. Many years may separate one legal matter and the next, or the commencement of litigation and its conclusion.

Quarterly Progress Report

The lawyer is in an unusual position, and continuing communications can be of special benefit to him. Since the development and final conclusion of a case may take several years, many attorneys lose contact with their clients. Because of this, the client may feel that his interests have been forgotten or neglected. Upon settlement of the case, some clients who receive a bill for professional services are disturbed by the fact that the bill seems out of proportion in relation to the time they feel has been spent by the attorney on the problem. The client fails to recognize that the attorney may devote considerable time each year on preparation of material. In situations such as this, it is the attorney's fault for failing to keep the client informed of work being done on the case.

I suggest that attorneys adopt a quarterly progress report which can be sent to all clients. This report need not be long or involved, but should simply relate activities which are taking place in the client's behalf. Not only will the progress report keep the client well informed, but it will also keep the name of the attorney ever prominent.

In his file, the professional man should have dates of special importance to his clients or patients, such as birthdays and anniversaries. There is little that engenders as much good will as being remembered on a special date. In fact, congratulatory messages on any special occasion are always well received. I suggest that a busy professional man employ a clipping service to scan local newspapers for items about clients or patients. The only thing you need to furnish a clipping service is a list of names. For a nominal fee, the service will watch for those names and supply you with any items appearing in print about them. The professional man can use this to great advantage if he will write a short, personal note of congratulations, attach the clipping, and forward it to the individual concerned.

Employ Clipping Service

In the area of continuing communication, the health care practitioner is in a unique situation. In recent years the public has become well aware of the importance of periodic health checkups and preventive medicine. In spite of this growing awareness, there are many practitioners who fail to get a large percentage of their patients to return after the initial visit. Part of the fault may lie in the fact that the practitioner has failed to sell himself and his profession **big** with the patient; and part of the fault may lie in the fact that he does not employ or understand the principles of an effective recall system.

Recall is the Key

In my concept of Administrative Public Relations, the recall system plays a key role. I am well aware of the fact that a practitioner cannot be successful if he retains only a small number of the new patients he sees each year. There is little point in employing all of the Administrative Public Relations principles that have been outlined if the practitioner cannot get the patient to return for a second visit.

Some may think that all a recall system involves is sending out a card indicating that it is time for a re-examination. Others may think that employing the principles of continuing communications will be sufficient. This is not true. The recall system is a technique unto itself, which if properly employed can bring about the desired results. A good recall system implements various pyschological motivations which should compel the patient to return for further care.

The recall card should be designed so that all the practitioner has to do is circle the day and month, write in the patient's name and the date and time of the appointment.

DR. GILBERT R. WEINER
OSTEOPATHIC PHYSICIAN
1020 N. E. 85th Street
Miami, Florida

Phone: 111-2222

M ______________________________

As you requested at the time of your last examination an appointment has been scheduled for you on . . .

MON.	TUES.	JAN.	FEB.	MAR.	APRIL
WED.	THURS.	MAY	JUNE	JULY	AUG.
FRI.	SAT.	SEPT.	OCT.	NOV.	DEC.

DATE ____________ TIME ____________

Making the Re-Appointment

The time to establish the need for a re-examination is during the examination itself. The patient should not leave the office before being told, fully and intelligently, the need for periodic re-examination and its relationship to proper health care. It is perfectly natural for a physician to say that, "While you're in excellent health today, it is wise to maintain a constant check on your physical condition." Or for a dentist or optometrist to give credence to the need for periodic examinations.

Many practitioners find it difficult to create the proper psychological attitudes necessary to stimulate the return of a patient. Here is the most successful method I have found for a doctor to use when approaching the patient:

"Mrs. Jones, during your examination we discussed the need for you to return in six months for a re-evaluation of your case. I know it is difficult for you to set a specific appointment, but since my schedule is quite heavy, I would like to block out some time for you now, say on January third. I know that this might not fit into your schedule then, but we will give you ample notice so that if it becomes necessary to change the date, you will be able to do so at that time. Does January third sound all right to you? Would you prefer an afternoon or morning appointment? All right then, let's put you down for 10 a.m. on January third. Mrs. Jones, would you mind addressing this envelope to yourself while I complete your record?"

At this point, the practitioner has at least scheduled an appointment for re-examination. There is an obvious advantage to this over that of first trying to obtain the appointment six months later through the use of card or phone.

A point to remember: This should only be done by the practitioner and not by his nurse or receptionist.

80 Per Cent Recall

Three weeks prior to the appointment for Mrs. Jones' re-examination, the practitioner should send a card reminding her that as a result of *her* conversation at the time of *her* last visit, a date has been set aside for her next appointment.

When she receives this notice, she will remember her last visit, since the envelope, in which the reminder came, will be addressed in her own handwriting. Psychologically, she will feel some obligation to the practitioner who has set aside valuable time for her and at her own request.

One week prior to Mrs. Jones' appointment, the practitioner's receptionist should phone her to confirm the date and time. By this time, Mrs. Jones feels an unusual obligation, first because she has set aside the time, and secondly because his office has taken additional time personally to confirm the appointment. Now, if Mrs. Jones cannot keep the appointment, she will most likely schedule a new one at a more convenient time.

Those who have employed this system at my suggestion tell me that they have achieved an 80 per cent recall.

Whether you are a young doctor or lawyer starting out in practice, or an established professional man building on it, one of the finest vehicles of public exposure open to you is a feature column in your local newspaper or magazine.

If you have any literary ability, and if your local magazine or newspaper is not already running a column encompassing your specific field—a health, financial or legal column written by you adds an immeasurable amount of prestige to your image and helps to create the public awareness that is vital to your success in the community.

If you are fortunate enough to obtain a column of your own, be sure that you discuss only items relating to your specialty. The recognition that you will obtain by writing the column should be sufficient reward. Do not attempt to use the column to promote your practice openly. You will create disfavor among your colleagues, the public and the publication.

Letters to the Editor

While we are discussing local newspapers and magazines do not overlook the opportunities offered by "letters-to-the-editor" columns. Your commentary on timely events relating to your field can be an important image builder.

Writing articles for your professional journal can also be a valuable tool, not only in building a reputation within your profession, but in gaining public recognition. Reprints of these articles, which can be understood by the layman, should be sent to your patients or clients.

Here are a few final ideas to be considered in building a professional image:

1. When you are called upon to deliver a speech before a group in your community, remember that your presentation can enhance your prestige or destroy your image. Be well prepared. Avoid talking over the heads of your audience, or with such deliberate authority that you give the impression of being pompous, overbearing, or long-winded. Your speech should be direct and to the point. If you do not have an innate talent for comedy, do not take on the role of a humorist.

If you are a poor speaker, you can still communicate effectively with your audience through the use of audio-visual aids. Enhance your talk with a motion picture on the subject matter, if one is available. At the conclusion of the film ask that questions be submitted to you on index cards which you have distributed prior to the showing of the film. You should now be able to handle these questions effectively and as result you will have given a meaningful and interesting program.

Not Too Many Index Cards

One last thought on this subject. I usually suggest that you slip-in a few index cards with questions of your own, covering subjects you wish to discuss. This will give you an opportunity to speak on questions which the audience may not pose. A word of caution if you do this: Be sure that you don't end up with more index cards than there are people in the audience.

2. Schedule your appointments far enough apart so that there is no undue waiting beyond the appointment time. Many professional men operate on the "drop-in-and-take-your-chances" principle. If the patient or client knows or is prepared for this he won't mind the wait. Nothing, however, will irk him more than to come to the office at the appointed time only to find several people and a long wait ahead of him.

Crowding the calendar may mean more immediate "business" but it eventually results in a loss of patients or clients.

3. Be careful to avoid over-exposure in local media. The professional man who has a news release sent out every time he leaves the office to attend a meeting, convention or seminar, will soon find that his patients or clients would rather he spend more time attending to their needs at home.

4. This brings us to another point, the use of the news release. I am not in favor of the professional man sending out his own releases to local media. If he does this himself, he will soon gain the reputation of "tooting-his-own-horn" and sooner or later these articles will not be carried by the local press. If he is attending a meeting or convention news releases should come from the sponsoring organizations.

What People Think You Are

Remember: your image is a reflection of what you are . . . perhaps more important . . . of what people think you are. Enhance that image at every opportunity. With the proper image, and with the inborn and learned skills you possess, you are destined to build your practice and *sell yourself big*.

H. W. GUROLNICK AND EARL D. EPSTEEN
Certified Public Accounts
4040 WEST LAWRENCE AVENUE
CHICAGO, ILLINOIS

February 11, 1966

Mr. Howard Thomas
1234 7th Ave.
New York, New York

Dear Howard:

I am pleased to send you the enclosed special tax and financial report. This will be the first of a series and I will send you one every month--strictly with my compliments, as a valued friend, and strictly for your profit and inside information, as part of my continuous financial service to you.

I believe you will find the report stimulating and rewarding. The articles are authoritative and reliable. They are designed to keep you up to the minute in your own tax and financial program. They are also an excellent way for me to keep in constant touch with you, so that I can be of greater service to you on changes, questions or problems you may have in any of the areas covered. If you have any question, just mark it off, and give me a call or drop me a line. I will do my best, as always, to help you in any of these financial planning areas.

Sincerely,

Earl D. Epsteen

/fr

Encl:

A personal letter explaining the new service should accompany the first professional newsletter sent to a patient or client.

ASSOCIATIONS

Nowhere else in the structure of free enterprise do we find such unrestricted opportunity for the businessman or the professional man to develop prestige and growth for himself and his profession, business or industry than in the association. Opportunities abound here in all directions.

The professional or industrial association has become an American institution.

Its prime function is to carry out specific activities for the benefit of its collective members—activities which the individual members cannot do for themselves or by themselves due to restrictions and limitations of time, talent, personnel or financial resources. Depending on the type or nature of the businessmen or professional men in an association, there are many and varied reasons for belonging to the association—many more than there are for not belonging.

It might be helpful to note what the largest association in the United States—the U.S. Chamber of Commerce—has to say about associations in its declared policy:

> . . . associations are an inherent part of the American democratic system. They provide a medium through which all members—from the

smallest to the largest—in any industry or profession may join forces for their common good . . . The flexibility of associations, their voluntary character, their freedom from special forms of government control, account in substantial degree for the benefits which have accrued from their cooperative work. Such conditions should be preserved in order that associations may continue to expand their usefulness to their fields of enterprise and to the public. The Chamber strongly urges upon American trade and professional men continued support for and participation in the work of their organizations.

Of the nation's nearly five million business firms, about four million, or 80 per cent, belong to one or more of the 13,000-plus recognized associations.

The Public Benefits, Too

From a properly functioning industrial association a businessman can expect help in solving management, product and distribution problems—and a myriad of other problems peculiar to the nature of single industries or trade fields.

Prime functions of an association today are to represent its membership in dealing with the many governmental agencies, and to prepare and project an effective program of public relations.

In this chapter, I offer some ideas for association management and for individual association members alike to stimulate public relations activities that will help them "Sell Themselves Big!"

Some of these ideas may be new to association workers, some may have been used, and some may be in effect right now. But every association should utilize anything and everything that will increase the prestige and good will of its members. The dollars a business or professional man spends for membership in his association should be returned many times over in greater profits. If this is not the case, it's time to find out why. Either he is not supporting his association, or it is not supporting him.

It is axiomatic that as the association benefits, the member benefits . . . and indirectly, the public benefits, too. The more effort and thought that is put into every phase of association work, the greater will be the rewards for its members. The more association meetings are approached with altruism, an open mind and a free exchange of ideas, the more progress will be achieved. This is particularly true of the work the association can do through public relations and in developing what I like to refer to as a "climate of awareness."

"Climate of Awareness"

A "climate of awareness" comprises the efforts of an association to focus the public's attention upon the profession or industry it represents. The association attempts to gain recognition, acceptance and respect for its individual members and their products or services. A "climate of awareness" for dental hygiene, for example, means that the public has been oriented to think of dentists when it thinks of oral hygiene and care of the teeth. The three become synonymous. The Aluminum Siding Association attempts to build a "climate of awareness" for the products its members market so that when Mr. and Mrs. Home Maker decide to remodel, they will purchase aluminum siding rather than steel, wood, clapboard, or masonry.

Neither the individual dentist nor the local XYZ Aluminum Siding executive can accomplish this by himself. It requires the concentrated efforts of an association promoting the services and products of all its members.

The two examples cited above pertain to two completely different types of associations. One is professional, the other industrial. Generally speaking, public relations plans at the association level apply to both, but it might be well to differentiate the two in our discussion. One comes under the category of public health and welfare, the other under private business enterprise. There are various programs that can be implemented for each.

For instance, an industrial association can advertise . . . a professional association rarely does. I speak primarily of general industry advertising conducted by an association. This, incidentally, comes as close to combining public relations with advertising as is possible. As I mentioned before, advertising and public relations are completely different tools; but the industry can advertise through an association in order to build an image for the industry, to build public acceptance for its products, and to court public favor for its causes.

Association Can Advertise

An aluminum association, comprised of prime producers of aluminum and the manufacturers of aluminum products, may conduct a national campaign to create a favorable "climate of awareness."

The railroads, in what they feel are justifiable stands against labor demands, may take their story to the public in the form of paid advertising in the newspapers. At the same time, labor unions have the same opportunities to use advertising space to present their side of a controversy.

Steel manufacturers may take TV network time, sponsoring newscasts to air the advantages of steel. They are not selling a specific steel product. They are merely building a "climate of awareness" for the many end products made of steel.

Messages of Interest

Professional associations, particularly those representing the health care fields, cannot do this without some risk to professional images. However, the professional association can take another route not open to the industrial. It can resort to the public education message, and can do this at a fraction of the cost of paid advertising. It is, in truth, performing a public service—actually contributing to the public welfare by offering messages of timely interest or health-protecting value. As such, the Federal Communications Commission welcomes these messages, and the radio and TV stations donate free time to such associations.

The various media benefit by building for themselves an image of willingness to donate space or time to worthy causes. The public benefits from more authoritative information. The association benefits by creating a "climate of awareness" for the services of its members.

Space Is Often Donated

It has become quite common for the TV viewer to hear words to the effect that "the following message is brought to you as a public service by this station in cooperation with the National Safety Council." . . . after which a one-minute spot on safe driving is presented. The American Optometric Association may be given public-service time to inform parents that Fall is back-to-school time, and then offer some good advice about eye care for children and the need for a complete professional eye examination.

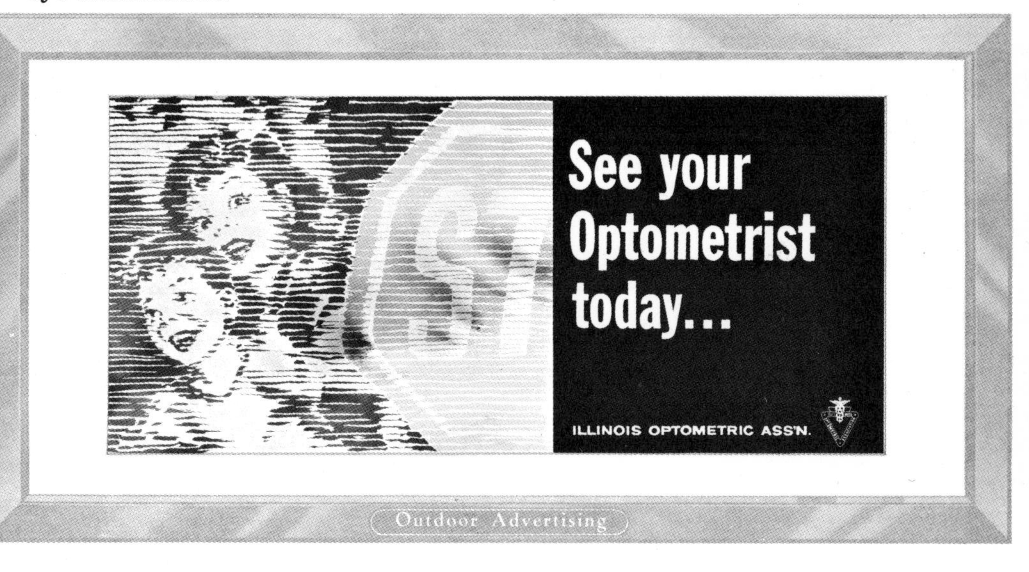

Billboard space is available to a non-profit professional association at no cost. All the association pays for are the production and posting charges.

Tax associations may offer some good tips on "how to save on your income tax" during the Spring of the year. Stations donate the air time. The public certainly benefits. If there is a "subliminal" message somewhere among the many points of advice, it might be the implication that you can benefit from consulting an accountant who is an expert in tax matters.

Similarly, a state bar association might provide newspapers with a column on "Your rights as a citizen." Efforts such as these help build public favor for the legal profession—a "climate of awareness"—and readers soon learn to appreciate the services of an attorney.

One medium more available to a professional association than to an industrial group is outdoor billboard space. Here again, as in the case with newspapers, TV and radio stations, space is often donated by an outdoor sign company to health professions or legal associations for public educational messages. The association is expected to pay the cost of producing the message and posting it, but considering the free billboard space and the impact on the thousands of people who are exposed to it, the cost-per-reader-reached becomes nominal.

An association exhibit can be an excellent public relations tool. It should be designed by an exhibit contractor to be of educational value in the field that the association represents.

Still another medium of exposure donated to professional associations is exhibit space. Many state and county fairs, auto shows, industrial conventions, school and community home shows will gladly provide free space to a professional association which has a timely educational or public service exhibit. Consider the thousands who attend a state fair and you'll realize that the cost of erecting the display amounts to a few pennies per viewer. Realize how much of a "climate of awareness" it develops for the association and the chances are, next time your association meets, you will recommend an educational exhibit at the next community or industrial show.

Bear in mind, however, that the display must carry a *bona fide* and altruistic message of interest to the public. Anything less, assuming such is accepted by the convention management, would appear commercial, do more harm than good and would degrade rather than enhance the association's professional image.

Bona Fide Presentation

Here are a few points to remember when constructing an exhibit.

1. Determine the message you wish to convey. Draft an outline of special points you want highlighted about your association and the field it represents.

2. Since the exhibit will be a representation of your association and membership, it should be professionally designed and constructed.

3. Most major cities have firms which specialize in the construction of exhibits. They can usually be found in the Yellow Pages of your local telephone book listed under "Exhibit Contractors."

Found in the Yellow Pages

4. Submit your outline to the exhibit contractor with an approximation of the budget your association has allocated for the exhibit. Request the contractor to submit a proposal to you in writing with a detailed copy of the plans.

5. Exhibits are large and bulky, even when they are designed to be shipped. Discuss arrangements with the contractor for storage and determine a fixed, monthly storage fee.

6. Check on the average costs for shipping, erecting and dismantling your exhibit at various shows. The exhibit contractor should be able to give you a good idea of extra costs involved.

7. Be sure that your association takes into consideration all the extra costs I have outlined and includes them in the total exhibit budget.

Now, there are several areas of public relations accessible to both the professional and the industrial association. One such area is the speakers bureau.

It has been truly said that, "an expert is a man who is away from home." This certainly applies to public speakers . . . and utilizing that idea here, the suggestion is to make every guest speaker someone who is "away from home."

For example, when the Lions Club looks for a guest speaker, it is far better to present a man from another town or city than a local Lions member or a local personality who is well-known to most of the membership.

The Expert Is Elsewhere

Every civic, social, fraternal and community organization is constantly on the alert for a good, informed speaker with a message, or speakers who are entertaining in one form or another. The program chairman is frequently hard-pressed to provide interesting speakers, meeting after meeting. Few of a group's own members have diversified or unusual occupations or subjects that will meet the program requirements. Those who do are quickly "used up," leaving the program chairman with the same problem. Here is where an alert association member can help out. A member who is a dentist can hardly volunteer to speak on dental hygiene. He might be accused of having a personal advantage interest. He is not "the expert" in the eyes of his community.

But he might volunteer to have Dr. Brown, a colleague from another area, appear as a lecturer on dental hygiene. Or he could volunteer to bring in a lecturer from the county dental society to speak on an interesting new development in dental health.

This is where the association comes into the picture BIG. In maintaining a panel of speakers who can be called upon to lecture to various organizations and civic groups, the association has a forceful and effective medium for extending its influence to many hundreds and even thousands of the public who otherwise might not hear the association's story.

This is an excellent public relations tool. It would be wise for the association to develop a large and diversified speakers bureau and to publicize its availability. The association can compile lists of all local organizations and announce the fact that it would be pleased to send a guest speaker to talk on a timely or provocative subject at a future meeting.

Speaker Has Captive Audience

The speaker, representing his association, has a captive audience. Again, he must be careful to avoid obvious commercialism or "selling." But representing his association as an authority, he has a marvelous opportunity to build an image and a "climate of awareness." Since the speaker can be an important asset to the association's public relations program, here are some suggestions for you to remember and to pass on to your membership when they are called upon to give speeches.

Another point—while also building the professional image, Dr. Brown is doing something newsworthy! "Last night Dr. A. J. Brown, of Cedar Point, spoke before the West Bend Lions Club on the timely subject of . . ." This is worthy of local editorial coverage. Now, bypassing the conventional advertising paths, which are closed to him, Dr. Brown has succeeded in getting his name and his profession into print.

Dr. Brown, the dentist, may not benefit directly from the speech he made that night, but Dr. Jones and all other dentists sitting in the audience might. Certainly, the dental profession will benefit from Dr. Brown's presentation. Remember, even if Dr. Brown, speaking away from his local community, doesn't benefit directly that night, he will when an exchange of speakers is made and Dr. Jones speaks before Dr. Brown's home audience.

The association should be sure to warn all of its members about two dangerous, and sometimes embarrassing, situations that frequently confront any guest speaker. The first is that every man is not a George Jessel. The man who can get up before a crowd, speak off the cuff and "leave them laughing" is indeed a rare find.

Visual help for lecture

To the man who is not the orator, who is more likely to leave them yawning, we suggest a few tried and tested aids. Almost every profession and industry has its own institutional motion pictures or sound-slide films. These are usually written, directed and filmed by professionals and are available through the association for local use. Such materials take the burden of elocution off the guest speaker. Or, the association can have a professionally created "flip-chart" using graphic illustrations to help cover the more significant points of the talk.

These visual aids are welcomed even by the accomplished speaker. There's a certain amount of drama and audience anticipation in the set-up movie projector or the closed flip-chart. As interesting as a speech might be, it is always improved by the use of visual aids.

Once the talk or movie has been concluded, the speaker faces the question-and-answer period. Experienced speakers recognize, and are frequently prepared for, this second danger point of the meeting. To the neophyte, or inexperienced speaker, it can be deadly.

You know the type

It seems that every audience, regardless of its nature or size, has its controversial character, the one who is always on his feet with a "stump-the-expert" question. His sole aim, it appears, is to throw guest speakers the curve ball, to smile broadly, and to wink knowingly at his neighbors while the speaker squirms. You know the type.

He can easily be evaded. Before the meeting begins, pass out "question cards" which will be picked up and passed on to you as soon as your talk is concluded. Announce that you will be happy to answer all the questions time will permit that are posed in this form. As the cards are passed to you, and as you glance through them, you will have time to screen them, eliminating those that are obviously attempting to "bait" you or those for which, embarrassingly enough, you may not have an answer.

You can even go one step further. If there is a tangent subject you wish to cover outside your organized talk, or questions you'd like to answer, write some cards of your own. It will help you keep the meeting at the level you wish and assure you and the audience of a successful question-and-answer period. Meeting a particularly reticent audience, you also avoid the blank stares and the blank cards which may terminate the meeting too abruptly.

There are other significant public relations activities that an association can perform for its individual members.

Producing the clip sheet

There's the "clip sheet," for example. The clip sheet is a periodic news-bureau type of release prepared and printed by an association and sent to all daily and weekly newspapers throughout the country or a specific area. It is usually printed in the form of a newspaper page and contains several articles pertaining to the field involved.

These articles can be straight news items, feature stories or short, general information items. While they contain information of general interest to the reading public, they are, of course, "slanted" to the best interests of the association's products or services.

The Asphalt Roofing Industry Bureau, for example, will produce a "clip sheet" on trends in building and construction. The sheet will contain various stories concerning the house and home. Interjected subtly in many of these articles are

NEWS BULLETIN

Vol. 8, No. 11 — November, 1965 — Chicago, Ill.

State of Texas Sets up Six Osteopathic Scholarships

FORT WORTH, TEXAS—The State of Texas has joined New York State in establishing scholarships for students attending out-of-state colleges of osteopathic medicine.

The Texas legislature in its recent regular session appropriated $9,600 for a two-year period to be paid to the colleges for tuition of students selected by the Texas Assn. of Osteopathic Physicians & Surgeons. In making the announcement, Dr. Elmer C. Baum, chairman, Public Health Committee of the Texas society, said that one-year scholarships of

Dr. Baum

$800 …
cants …
achie…
denc…
uate…
Fu…
nati…
Uni…
able…
cal …
me…
F…
of …
six…
ne…
ye…
se…
a…
j…
a…

Adopt Research & Training Centers, More Aid to Osteopathic Colleges

Congress Passes Reduced Plan to Fight Heart Disease, Cancer & Stroke; New Improvement Grants for Colleges

WASHINGTON, D.C.—Two landmark laws breaking new ground in medical research & training centers and in federal aid to osteopathic and medical colleges were enacted by the Congress in October.

Both bear the disarming title of amendments to earlier acts, although they set new precedents and launch new programs of far-reaching effect.

The federal government undertakes a much broader program of grants to osteopathic and medical schools for improving the quality of education. The college assistance amendments (HR 3141) also extend for three years the program of grants for construction and … and medical …

Health Professions Educational Assistance Act.

The new amendments also authorize scholarships for osteopathic and medical students from low-income families of up to $2,000 for 10% of all students of a school, beginning with the freshman classes in 1966, and proceeding by classes, step by step, to cover 10% of all students by 1969.

… Cancer & Stroke

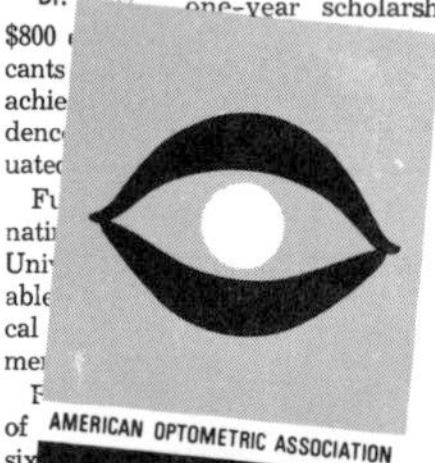

NATIONAL AFFAIRS BULLETIN

EXCLUSIVELY FOR KEYMEN

AMERICAN OPTOMETRIC ASSOCIATION

WASHINGTON OFFICE, 1026 SEVENTEENTH STREET, N. W.

WASHINGTON, D. C. 20036

Phone (202) 783-4010

January 6, 1966
89-28

SUBJECT: A revised bill for the practice of optometry in the District of Columbia.

SUMMARY: This is a completely rewritten law for the practice of optometry in the District of Columbia. The original law passed by Congress in 1924 has never been amended. It is hopelessly inadequate and antiquated. An example is the following existing definition of the profession:

"That the practice of optometry is defined to be the application of optical principles through technical methods and devices in the examination of the human eye for the purpose of determining visual defects and the adaption of lenses for the aid and relief thereof."

The current controls of the Board of Optometry over a license are limited to:

"The conviction of crime involving moral turpitude, habitual use of narcotics, or any other substance which impairs the intellect and judgement to such an extent as to incapacitate anyone for the duties of optometry, or for a conviction as provided in section 2 of this Act". Section two of the Act makes it a misdemeanor for a person to hold himself forth as an optometrist unless he has passed a "limited examination" and received a license to practice optometry.

The applicant to qualify …
on …

features and benefits of asphalt roofing. Frequently there will be an article specifically on asphalt roofing, released because of its news value and the fact that it can stand by itself as a legitimate news article.

In writing the clip sheet, be careful not to make its purpose too obvious. This is not an advertising copywriting job. Each article must appear as if it were written by a newspaper itself, relating the unembellished facts of a situation. Doing more than that is "editorializing," and your chances of having the story published diminish accordingly.

The editor of the "home building" section likes to get this material—as does the editor of the small town newspaper. They often find it difficult to fill their columns continuously with genuine home or building news. It is always excellent "filler."

Benefits to the association are obvious. The industry it represents gets invaluable, free, editorial exposure, and every article that appears creates a closer "climate of awareness" in the public's mind toward a specific product or industry.

Folders and brochures

Another program that an association can utilize for its members is printed literature. With funds for such projects, and hired professionals preparing good material, the association can produce effective folders and brochures upon which the individual member's name can be imprinted. This makes the folders appear as if they were produced by that member, yet they are available to him at a fraction of what he would pay if he had to produce the piece himself.

Still another association project is the issuance of news bulletins, interesting articles and informative letters concerning the profession or trade,

The association newsletter to members is a *must* for keeping the members informed of current happenings.

The legislative bulletin, sent by the association to "key men" involved in political work, is a good way to communicate.

keeping professional businessmen abreast of the changing times. This is vital, in that the professional man is now better informed and can volunteer information to his patients or clients regarding trends in his field.

Merchandising vehicle

As a corollary to the supply line of information, many associations publish trade or professional journals. It is printed under association auspices, members contribute articles, new findings, innovations in their field. Editors supplement these articles with news reporting of their own. Advertising is obtained from suppliers to the association members. If the magazine is not a profit-maker, it is at least self-sustaining.

However, a poorly produced or poorly managed magazine can harm the association's image. If an association does not feel that it has the facilities to publish its own magazine successfully, it may do well to look for an independent publishing concern and work out some sort of cost-plus basis for having a journal published professionally.

The convention is an additional public relations function carried on at the association level. Often it is combined with an exhibition. The convention's purpose is to hold business meetings and workshops for group members.

An exhibition permits suppliers and manufacturers to display their new products. As such, the "show phase" of the program is an advertising and merchandising vehicle for both the firms that serve the association and for the association members themselves.

The association exhibit creates a "climate of awareness" throughout the field. Seminars and workshops permit the association to call upon its own and outside experts to speak to the members on latest trends, suggested systems, and latest techniques and developments. In performing this service, the association also builds its own image.

This is certainly true of industrial trade shows.

The professional association convention has its vital effect, too. An osteopathic seminar, for example, is conducted by the profession's association and is restricted to osteopaths only. They are not trying to impress the general public with the importance of their function or services. Such professional seminar, then, is designed for education and improvement. The speaker talks to other osteopaths concerning research findings, new or improved methods and experiments in new procedures.

While the professional seminar is primarily an instructive program, let us not forget the direct public relations mileage that the association and the individual member can obtain from it. The professional attending a seminar in a distant city warrants mention in his hometown newspaper. Again, we have uncovered an instance by which a lawyer, doctor or accountant can get his name into print on the basis of genuine news value.

The association should perform this public relations service for the member by using a standard mimeographed form on which the news item is already written. All that is required is to fill in the blanks left for the name of the attending professional man, his address and hometown or city, whereupon the story should be mailed to the man's hometown newspaper.

Delicate area of politics

One of the most delicate areas of association activity is politics—local, state and national.

Important legislation is frequently influenced by the political action arm and general weight and prestige of a large association.

For that reason and because professional and industrial associations should be constantly alert to legislation activity which may affect their fields of operation or interest, each association needs a "political action" or legislative committee under the direction or guidance of a chairman experienced in politics.

Politics takes many strange and devious turns, and it is not my intention to cover all of its specific practices. Instead, here is some concrete advice on the subject of elections and association "support" for party or independent candidates.

1. Ideally, an association should not become openly involved in local, state or national elections by actively supporting one party against another. Whatever the outcome, the association which has done so is certain to lose externally and internally. The best interests of the association members should always be kept uppermost in mind, and this dictates that an association must remain out of active or open party campaigning.

Better to work for incumbent

2. However, an association can support an incumbent candidate whose political philosophies closely parallel the association's policies. This candidate deserves to be supported by the association and by the individual members. The association, in this case, should play a role of leadership by informing membership that the candidate has been a close "friend," and by helping individual members organize a campaign effort for the candidate.

3. Encourage your members to prepare—when they can do so without hurting their own businesses or practices—letters to be sent to customers or patients in support of the candidate.

4. One thing for an association to remember is that it is always better to support an *incumbent* candidate, if he has worked in the association's best interests. It is a fact of political life that the incumbent has an advantage over his opponent. If the opponent does win, he will respect your loyalty to the defeated incumbent and he will expect that same loyalty. If a politician has been outspoken in his views against the association, the association should actively campaign against him. You have the right to seek representation that reflects your point of view. Also, there is nothing to lose and everything to gain if this man is defeated.

5. Never enter a primary fight. No matter who wins, you lose. If you support a Republican against a Republican in a primary fight and your man loses, you have alienated not only the successful Republican candidate but also the Democratic candidate.

6. Before and during an election the association should circulate campaign information to its members, information that explains the candidate's background, platform, positions on past bills, and aid or opposition that he has given to the association.

7. Shortly after the election is over, the association should send an official letter of congratulations to each elected officeholder. This letter should refer, by name, to the association member or members in his district or state who worked actively for his election.

8. A list of members who are personally acquainted with each of the elected officials is one of the most important files in the political armament of an association. These are the members who should be called upon whenever the association requires a contact with a legislator for any reason of association interest. In the case of a professional association, such as the American Medical Association, discover who is the legislator's physician, then use this man as a contact to the legislator. Letters from constituents bring faster action and carry more weight than official association correspondence—although such correspondence has its own degree of impact.

Keep in Close Contact

Once having compiled this list of "key men" it is necessary to keep in close contact with them. A legislative newsletter is one of the best ways of circulating information and keeping "key men" up to date on current legislation.

It might be pointed out here that political candidates and office holders form their impressions of industrial professional groups from their personal contact with members of the industry or profession. This is almost certain to take its initial impetus from those local constituents who aid the candidate in his campaign or who, in one manner or another, become personally acquainted with him. Thus, the "climate of awareness" is usually established early, and it is wise for the association to maintain it for as long as the office holder remains in a position of political influence.

One highly recommended procedure for keeping the good will of office holders is the local, state or national association dinner or convention to which a number of selected legislators and influential politicians are invited as guests — with appropriate introductions and acknowledgements. The same principle is involved in local golf outings and picnics. Invite as many political personalities as can be afforded. Give them all complimentary tickets. Nothing will hurt you more than to invite prominent politicians and expect them to pay. They should be your guests—all the way.

On the other side of the fence do not forget the political dinner or social gathering. Be sure your association buys tickets, and be sure that you are represented. The small sums you expend at these gatherings will engender much good will, and will help the candidate meet some of his campaign expenses.

Don't Abuse Press Conference

The idea of holding a general press conference is much abused by many associations—almost as much as it is by large corporations and amateur public relations people working for various organizations and conventions.

Too many public relations people still believe that a so-called "press conference" with hors d'oeuvres and copious alcoholic beverages will put a gloss on their news handouts and make them more palatable. They fail to realize that, first, the reporter covering the session is not the final authority or judge of what will be printed; second, editors of metropolitan newspapers, mass circulation magazines, and national press associations will not be influenced by the gloss or alcohol—only by the newsworthiness of the event or announcement.

Some large associations use the press conference routine at their state or national conventions—most of them not too wisely. A few points ought to be kept well in mind before a press conference is scheduled and before inadvertent statements or actions cause irreparable damage:

Don't hold a press conference if it's for the sole purpose of handing out press releases or just pleasing the association president or someone else in authority. Neither of these reasons satisfies the requirements of a press conference, and will waste the time of reporters or specialty writers who may show up expecting something of an unusual nature which could not be conveyed through the use of an ordinary press release.

The "name" is valid

A valid reason for holding a press conference is the presence of a nationally known personality—a recognized "name" in government, industry, science, military or other field of endeavor and whose news value is genuine or timely. There are other good reasons linked to product innovations, professional discoveries, health advancements, policy statements on national issues, etc. A telephone call or advance letter to the various media should be considered when a valid news interview is planned.

Remember that a press conference is basically designed to give news personnel a chance to talk with the principal—the person being interviewed—about a matter which the press believes to be newsworthy, or to see an unusual demonstration or exhibit that cannot adequately be explained with words.

Prepare fact sheets

If you expect the press to cover the event at your request, be prepared to have some news releases and "fact sheets" regarding the subject and the association. Not too many reporters these days take shorthand well enough (if at all) to get everything down factually or to get exact quotes. If your association has specialized terminology or technical functions, fact sheets will help reporters get unusual words and names spelled correctly.

For association personnel or public relations men, there is only one general rule for a press conference —provide information in an objective manner and in a manner which will make it easy for the press to get the right picture.

Frequently, a film or slide presentation — or other visual aid—serves to give the press a better and more controlled picture of the association's message. These are especially good for scientific or technical presentations. However, on film presentations—offer them early—not at the conclusion of a talk or interview, because films at the conclusion make it easy for the press to slip out. Keep the press in sight at all times.

College and high school press conferences

For some of the larger associations—particularly those of professional or scientific nature—it is well to hold college and high school press conferences to which local journalism students are invited. This is good experience for both the students and for the association as it gives the youngsters a chance to interview prominent educators, scientists, professional men and others. It also helps smooth out some of the wrinkles in preparing for the conference with the working press. In addition, such conferences are helpful in informing future journalists as to the nature and function of the association and its members.

If *image* is a reflection of what an individual is, then the image of the association is a reflection of the entire field. Through every phase of a well-conducted and implemented public relations program, the association endeavors to reflect properly upon itself. In so doing, the individual member's image is enhanced. There is much more that the association can do as a body than the member can possibly do as an individual. If a "climate of awareness" is to be created for a specific profession or a specific industry, it can be done only at the association level, with combined effort, combined finances and combined programs.

An image is a reflection

WELCOME

MUNICIPALITIES

CIVIC GOVERNMENT PUBLIC RELATIONS

We have discussed the feasibility of the individual altering his image through Administrative Public Relations. We have seen how this can be done for the small businessman, the professional, the public office seeker, and the educator. We have seen the practical application of Administrative Public Relations efforts at work in molding the image of the group, the association and the chamber of commerce. But, can these same principles be applied to a task affecting thousands or even millions? Can one change the face and the spirit of an entire city?

Although difficult, it can, and has been done by Richard J. Daley, mayor of the city of Chicago. In this chapter I will explore some of Mayor Daley's basic principles and philosophies, applied so well in changing the international image of his city. Then, I will take the same program and show how it can be adapted to the needs of the small village, town or city.

To translate the job that Mayor Daley did into advice for smaller communities and to understand Chicago's transformation, one must understand the man behind it. It is an interesting story—one that merits attention.

Chicago Tribune Photo

Mayor of Chicago, Richard J. Daley, looks over the city that he helped to rebuild.

Richard J. Daley was born of hard working immigrant parents in a modest neighborhood on Chicago's South Side. As a youngster, he sold newspapers just a few blocks from where he lives today. After high school, he took a job in Chicago's stock yards, and attended DePaul University at night. He was graduated from law school in 1933, and passed the bar examination that same year. In 1936 he married Eleanor Guilfoyle and is now the father of seven children.

His modest beginning had a profound impression upon him. Even to this day, he keeps in close touch with his neighbors. Still living in his old neighborhood, he remains active in his local church and the many civic, social and fraternal organizations of his community.

He Carries a Torch

Richard J. Daley carries a torch. He maintains a sincere love affair with his city. When he first took office as Mayor, he was frustrated in this "love." He was convinced that Chicago was the world's greatest city, but he could find few to agree with him. How could he convince others?

Chicago had stagnated through two wars and a depression. Economic hardships had left the city devoid of modern facilities. Street lighting was antiquated, traffic control was poor, the city was unkempt and depressing, the police and fire departments were inadequate; and worse, Chicago had been internationally branded with a reputation for rampant gangsterism. The spirit had left the city.

Before he could rebuild Chicago's image, he had to rebuild Chicago.

Off the Drawing Boards

To launch a comprehensive program of capital improvements, he needed millions of dollars in additional revenue. Enlisting the aid of all local media and civic groups, Mayor Daley sold his dream of Chicago to its people. They responded by giving him their confidence, approving the largest bond issues in the city's history.

Now he could begin. New lighting was installed on every block, automatic street cleaning equipment was pressed into service, and the functions of municipal departments were reviewed and updated. The job was thorough. Chicago soon took on a new look.

This was just the start. Modern traffic control systems were installed. Superhighway construction was accelerated. All of this was in line with Mayor Daley's philosophy that, "Blueprints for better living mean nothing unless something is actually done to get them off the drawing boards."

One of the biggest tasks confronting the Daley administration was to eliminate the crime and corruption that had given the city such a bad name. After a major police scandal that erupted soon after he took office, Mayor Daley obtained the services of the country's leading criminologist—O. W. Wilson.

The new police superintendent was shielded from political pressures, was given unrestricted authority and the Mayor's unqualified backing. Among the reforms and new police methods that he initiated,

Superintendent Wilson embarked upon an extensive public relations program. This program was designed not only to inform Chicago citizens of the protection which was available to them and the progress which had been made by the police department, but also to solicit the aid of citizens in fighting crime.

Orlando Wilson's public relations program, which utilized newspaper, radio and television coverage, made citizens aware of the massive changes which had taken place within the police department. A 40-foot, mobile display unit was constructed. This exhibit cruiser toured the city, stopping at busy traffic intersections to explain the many programs involved in the operation of the Chicago Police Department. Other exhibits also were designed, making the same points as the mobile cruiser, to be used at all large conventions held in Chicago.

Next, Mr. Wilson set out to enlist the aid of the citizen in crime prevention. "Operation Crime Stop" was organized. This program asked Chicagoans to "lend their eyes and ears" in reporting suspicious activities immediately to the police department. "Operation Crime Stop" was publicized in all media and a series of posters was circulated throughout the city. This program was extremely successful.

Model of Excellence

Today, Chicago's Police Department is one of the finest. It is a model, studied by law enforcement bodies from all over the world—from England's Scotland Yard to the Japanese police force.

Also undertaken by Mayor Daley were programs to improve fire protection, sub-standard housing, and health and welfare.

Another area of concentration was transportation. Chicago participated actively in the program to develop the St. Lawrence Seaway, opening Chicago's waterways to ocean traffic and enabling the city to become an international seaport. Under Mayor Daley, Chicago designed and built O'Hare

CITY OF CHICAGO / DEPARTMENT OF POLICE 1121 South State Street Chicago, Illinois 60605 WAbash 2-4747

RICHARD J. DALEY, *Mayor*
O. W. WILSON, *Superintendent*

OPERATION CRIME-STOP

The Chicago Police request all law-abiding citizens to join Operation Crime-Stop.

WHAT is Operation Crime-Stop? It is the new crime prevention campaign to increase public cooperation with Chicago Police in reporting suspicious events occurring in and around business places, homes, residences and parks.

HOW does Operation Crime-Stop work? Whenever citizens see or hear something suspicious, they are urged to call the Police emergency telephone number PO 5-1313. You can give the dispatcher your name and address or remain anonymous as you wish. There is no telephone charge for emergency

Some of the city-wide publicity done by the Chicago Police Department to introduce Operation Crime Stop.

International Airport—the world's largest and most heavily used air terminal. Interestingly enough, this ultra-modern air facility did not cost the Chicago taxpayer any money. The building bonds which were issued for construction are being retired by the commercial airlines that use the field.

The Chicago Department of Forestry was instrumental in beautifying the city. New trees and flowers were planted all over Chicago. The park district was encouraged to enlarge its facilities, including parks, zoos, fieldhouses, bathing beaches, and outdoor and indoor swimming pools.

A City's Grand Opening

McCormick Place, one of the world's largest convention facilities under one roof, was built to maintain Chicago's position as "Convention Capital of

Top: Mobile police exhibit cruiser designed by the Chicago Police Department to show the citizens of Chicago how the police department operates. Bottom: The central control room of the Chicago Police Department is completely computerized to increase the effectiveness of police protection in the giant city.

the World." This modern exhibit hall boasts more attendance and more events than any similar exposition center.

For its citizens' cultural enjoyment, city museums were publicized; and attendance at outdoor concerts and at Chicago's own symphony orchestra and opera was encouraged.

The spirit of the people began to improve. Private enterprise took the initiative. Old buildings were cleaned and rehabilitated. Owners were encouraged to illuminate large buildings to enhance the beauty of the city skyline.

Once the internal shortcomings of the city had been rectified—only four years after Mayor Daley took office—Chicago was ready to be shown to the world.

Richard J. Daley decided that it was time to hold a "grand opening" for his new and beautiful city. He approached the State Department, in Washington, D. C., to have Chicago placed on the federal government's V.I.P. list of stops for international visitors. This was done.

Chicago's American Photo

Red Carpet for the Queen

Chicago was ready for its debut.

Through the efforts of the Daley administration, arrangements were made for Her Majesty, Queen Elizabeth II of England, to visit the city. After her tour of Canada, Chicago would be the only United States city visited by the Queen.

A great deal of time, money and planning went into preparing for Her Majesty's visit. I was a member of the Mayor's staff at the time; arrangements were time-consuming and arduous. The Queen was scheduled to spend a day in Chicago, a day to be filled with receptions, tours of cultural and historic sites, and a final grand banquet during the evening. This required perfect organization and split-second timing.

Chicago's American Photo

The reception that was given to England's Queen Elizabeth II helped to revitalize the spirit of the city of Chicago.

Few such receptions could exceed that which Chicago accorded its royal visitor that day. Ambassadors stationed in the United States from all the Commonwealth nations came to greet their Queen. Each left with a new impression of Chicago.

As Queen Elizabeth's royal barge landed at the city's lakefront, cannons along the shore fired a 21-gun salute; British and United States flags floated down over the harbor and the heraldic trumpets of the President's personal corps played "Hail Brittania." The Queen walked down a red carpet between the diplomatic reviewing stands and proceeded to a podium where she extended her greetings to the people of Chicago and the United States. She then entered a waiting limousine and led a grand parade through the heart of the city. The entire day passed with impressive speed. As the Queen's barge departed after the banquet a tremendous display of fireworks filled the sky overhead.

Tuned in to Chicago

The visit of a reigning monarch to Chicago had accomplished three things: 1. An internationally famous sovereign had been impressed by the beauty, culture and administration of Chicago; 2. The importance and beauty of the occasion had re-instilled in Chicago citizens a feeling of community pride and spirit; and 3. The attention of the international press had been focused on the city. Every aspect of Chicago, from the most basic information about the city itself to the final coverage of the Queen's visit, had been reported to the world.

Richard J. Daley had realized his lifelong ambition. He had remolded his city so that it deserved to be visited by one of the world's most beloved figures. The miles of movie film shot, the thousands of photographs taken, and the volume of words written, were seen and read everywhere. A new image of Chicago had been created in the eyes of the world.

Since the visit of Queen Elizabeth II to Chicago,

other great world dignitaries have *asked* to have Chicago put on their itineraries as they toured the United States.

Following the Queen's visit, Chicago played host to the Pan-American Games; from all over Latin-America and Canada came athletes to participate in sporting events; this also helped to publicize the city and to boost the morale of its citizens.

The world was tuned in to Chicago. National magazines and newspapers began to look at the city in a new light, and media coverage resulted automatically. I began to moderate a weekly radio show called "This is Chicago." On the program I covered the "people, places and events that make Chicago the world's most exciting city." Nationally known personalities were interviewed, and events such as meetings, conventions, theatrical performances and concerts were reported in interesting feature style. Although primarily local, a few of my more important interviews were aired by national networks. Chicago was on the move!

Richard J. Daley's "love affair" with Chicago had been consummated. He had brought a new meaning, spirit and vitality to his city. The image of Chicago had been changed. The exodus of residents to the city's suburbs had been stemmed. New building projects had been initiated. The citizen with grown children returned to the city seeking the services and conveniences which it now offered. New and diversified industry was again attracted. The family unit returned to Chicago to find it a better, healthier and safer place in which to live, work, worship and play. The city had revitalized itself, and the downward trend had been reversed.

But Many Do Not

The principles which Mayor Richard J. Daley utilized in changing the image of Chicago can be applied to any small city, town or village.

It goes without saying that not every town is in need of a complete "face lifting." Many towns have fine community expansion and planning programs. Many towns have good public relations campaigns to attract new residents and new industry—**but, many do not.**

There are several signs that can betray a declining community. The most obvious of these are population decrease, empty stores, and lack of new construction. This is all part of a pattern which is evident in every dying community. When a city fails to attract new industry or when established commerce begins to leave, families soon depart because of lack of employment. As the population moves out, the position of the commercial interests weakens, and many stores begin to close as businessmen begin to seek environments more conducive to trade. With the departure of industry and commerce and a large segment of the population, the doctor, lawyer and accountant soon find that there no longer exist sufficient patients or clients to sustain practices—they, too, depart. The city, now devoid of much of its commerce, industry and professional men, finds it almost impossible to attract new people.

Thus, you have the "death of a city."

In order to revive the dying city, it is necessary to go back to the beginning of the decline cycle, to the basic cause—industry's exodus. You must ascertain what caused industry to become dissatisfied with the community. Finding these conditions, you must correct them before you can re-attract other industry and rebuild the city.

A Complex Situation

There are a multiplicity of interrelated factors that cause industry to move out of a community. It is a complex situation. Understand that each factor affects the other; and that it is extremely difficult to pin down any ONE cause. It is a which-came-first-the-chicken-or-the-egg question. For example: if a town fails to have a community climate favorable to family life, people begin to move out. Without adequate local manpower, industries are forced to move to other areas. If, on the other hand, industry finds the climate such that it cannot continue to operate, it relocates, and the families, faced with unemployment, must also leave.

Some of the factors which create unfavorable conditions for industry are:

1. *Zoning*—A city, through its zoning laws, must maintain a healthy balance between industrial and residential areas. If you become overly restrictive to industry in your zoning laws; if these laws prohibit expansion and business growth, then industry eventually will be forced to relocate. If you haven't taken measures to protect the residential characteristics of the community, then families become dissatisfied.

Don't "Bleed" Industry

2. *High taxes*—If a city creates a tax structure which tends to "bleed" industry in disproportion to the other contributors to the general tax fund—small business, property owners and consumers—again, industry will be forced to seek new areas.

3. *Poor government* — Poorly managed civil government, corruption, or lack of progressive leadership will discourage industry. Industry expects local government to provide sound, long-range community planning, effective police protection, and other municipal services.

4. *Transportation facilities*—The end result of all industrial effort is the product. Once completed, the product must be distributed to outlying markets. Local government must recognize this. If the products are primarily transported by trucks, local government should not pass unfair traffic ordinances that hamper this process. If air transportation is needed, the local municipality should work with the federal government to obtain airport facilities that meet the needs of industry.

What can a community, which has deteriorated, do to re-attract industry, commerce and people?

Before the community can extol its virtues through public relations, it must first adhere to the basic precepts of Administrative Public Relations; and, as Mayor Richard J. Daley did, solve its internal problems.

Provide Basic Security

Since industry depends upon manpower, the city must create an atmosphere conducive to family living.

1. Give families the basic security of effective, efficient and honest police and fire protection.

2. Many municipal services must be provided by the local government to help maintain a healthy residential atmosphere: refuse must be removed regularly; a health department should be established, competently staffed and operated to safeguard residents; streets, sidewalks and alleys should be maintained in a good state of repair; general traffic control should be efficient and modern, and streets should be well lighted.

3. Good, modern and conveniently located educational facilities are vital for attracting the family to the community. The method by which these can be obtained was discussed in a previous chapter.

4. The city must provide parks, playgrounds and supervised recreational facilities for all the members of a family. Areas should be set aside for both the quiet family picnic and for sports activities.

5. Warmth, beauty and culture are essential parts of a healthy city, conducive to family living. Cities, towns and villages should not be composed solely of stone and concrete. Well organized reforestation programs which result in tree-lined streets and avenues, and well maintained park and play areas should be instituted. Home gardening and landscaping should be encouraged. All of this contributes to city beautification.

Culture plays an important part in community life and the city has an obligation to encourage its

Top: To make Chicago a "place where people want to live" cultural events are held throughout the year. During the Summer months afternoon and evening concerts can be heard at the Grant Park band shell. Bottom: McCormick Place, one of the largest exposition centers in the world attracts millions of conventioners every year.

development. Well planned and administered library facilities are important. Also, the city should stimulate and sponsor, when possible, groups such as: symphony orchestras, flower and garden clubs, art fairs and drama groups.

Once the "climate" is such that families will again be attracted to the community, industry's "manpower problem" will be solved.

For Attractive "Climate"

When the city's internal problems have been corrected the next step is the formation of a citizens committee, composed of governmental, commercial and industrial leaders. The primary purpose of this committee is to sell the advantages of

A perfect example of city beautification for the enjoyment of residents and visitors is Chicago's waterfront and Grant Park.

the city to industries located elsewhere. The committee should be armed with such incentives as tax benefits, favorable zoning, and relocation sites. The expenses of the committee can be met on an equal participation basis by both government and private enterprise.

1. In selling new industry on relocating in its city, the committee should be able not only to assure the industry of an equitable tax structure, but should, in many cases, be able to offer such incentives as reduced taxes or tax-free land for a period of years to help defray the cost of relocation.

2. The committee should be able to present a comprehensive plan of the city which will show long-range programs for community development—with particular emphasis on industrial zoning. The plant that relocates will want to be sure of a climate conducive to its future growth and expansion.

3. Many communities, in attempting to attract new industry, make sites available at costs somewhat less than their actual market value. The difference in the actual land costs are sometimes borne by public and private contributions.

4. Besides incentives, the committee should also be armed with impressive brochures and pamphlets emphasizing all the points I made previously relating to health, community and family life, favorable laws and tax structures.

And a City Is Re-Born

Some of the most successful communities in the United States are those which stimulate pride and loyalty, not only among the general populace but among commerce and industry as well. Residents, businessmen and industrial corporations seek to fulfill their requirements for goods and services from within their own localities.

Working with the chamber of commerce, representatives of the industrial firms, and civic organizations, the city should develop a program to make its citizens aware of the goods and services that are available. Developing this type of loyalty will aid in building pride and spirit.

Once the community has revitalized itself, the upward cycle should begin again. As industry returns, it attracts workers and their families who find that the community now offers more desirable family living. With the return of the people, their basic need for goods and services stimulates commerce. And, with flourishing industry, increasing population and expanding commerce, the professional man now finds a healthful climate in which to practice.

Thus, a city is re-born.

POLITICAL CANDIDATES

The public's conception of the task of a political candidate is really a public misconception. There's a great deal more to running for office than making speeches, smiling for photographers and kissing babies. If you are inclined toward 16-hour work periods, sleepless nights and fretful days, you are prepared to enter the political arena. But, lest this picture prove a deterrent to your political ambitions, let me hasten to add that counterbalancing such tribulations is an excitement, an exhilaration and a gratification—win or lose—found in no other activity.

There is no other field of activity in which public relations, in its most direct form, plays a more important role. Running for office *is* public relations in action. It is your relation to the voting public; your ability to reflect a proper image; your power to mold public opinion and to motivate the voters to go to the polls, that eventually determine the outcome of the election.

It all started, of course, with George Washington. He created the image. He did this through his own efforts, through the life he led, his trials and successes, his personal deeds. The high-powered press agent, the high-pressure mass media and the smoothly-operating public relations firm were not available to him. He did it all himself.

Each political candidate who followed, whether he ran for the presidency or in a local mayoral race, attempted to build the image that would win the election for him. So, through the years Washington became known as the man who could not tell a lie. Stephen Douglas became the "little giant," Lincoln was "Honest Abe," and William Jennings Bryan was the "silver tongued orator."

Hole in the Shoe

Adlai Stevenson will be remembered for his achievements, but when history records his political career, it will envision a photograph of this affluent gentleman, sitting slumped in his chair with a hole in the sole of his shoe. This photo of Mr. Stevenson was printed in hundreds of newspapers and was seen by millions of readers. The photo helped change the public's concept of him from that of an intellectual untouchable to a man of humility.

Our politically ambitious ancestors had no mass media as a public relations tool. In the earthy democracy of the country's early days, the candidate met face-to-face with his electorate. His image was built through direct contact, through the personality, character and mannerisms he exposed to the public.

With the advent of mass communications the political campaign changed. Theodore Roosevelt was one of the first presidents who learned to use newspapers as an effective public relations tool. The first proponent of the use of radio, the one at least who used it most effectively until that time—was Franklin D. Roosevelt. He used the radio "fireside chat" to deliver his message directly to the public. His "chats" became a national habit. Millions would gather about their radios to hear the warm, ingratiating "My Friends" opening to his chat. And more people than ever before in our

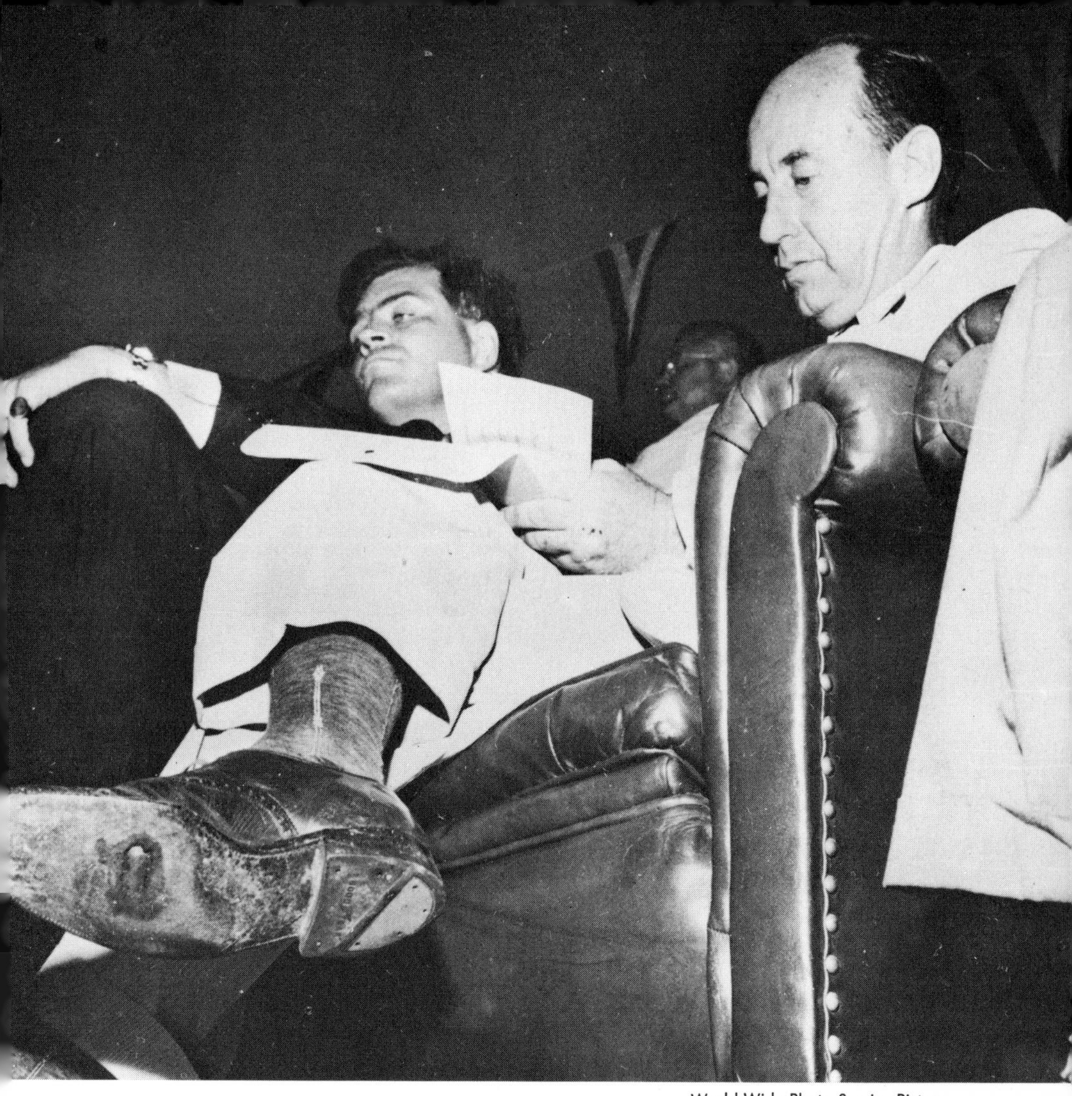

World Wide Photo Service Picture
This internationally famous picture of the hole in Adlai Stevenson's shoe changed his image overnight.

history would know what their President was thinking, planning, doing.

He built an image through those fireside chats. He developed confidence in him and his administration. He bolstered the courage of the millions who had been demoralized by the world's most disastrous economic depression. No political opponent, no matter how strong, could shake that image, nor have the slightest chance of victory when Mr. Roosevelt ran for re-election.

In 1960, another new form of mass communications played a vital part in a presidential election. Television was now a household item and the

Narrowest of Margins

politically seasoned Vice-President Richard Nixon and the young Senator John F. Kennedy agreed to use this medium to debate the issues. The country was pretty evenly divided. Mr. Kennedy won by the narrowest of margins. Few can doubt the impact television had on the outcome of this election.

This one brief chapter on running for public office in a book dealing with all phases of public

World Wide Photo Service Picture

President Franklin D. Roosevelt was one of the first presidents to make effective use of the medium of radio for purposes of communication. His "Fireside Chats" were heard in almost every home in the nation.

relations is not meant to be a complete treatise on the subject. Volumes can be written on how to conduct a successful political campaign.

What I am offering are some basic guidelines for those who want to seek public office. If you are campaigning or considering campaigning, chances are, you are seeking a local office. Other than free news coverage, mass media are either not available to you or are too expensive.

This being the case, your political campaigning more nearly parallels that of our country's earliest office seekers than it does present-day candidates running for national office. Yours is the task of direct personal contact . . . of SELLING YOURSELF BIG, face-to-face with your constituents. What I offer are some basic mechanics, adequate guidelines and helpful hints that may aid you in your efforts. Keys to a successful venture into politics are communications and organization.

The candidate must avail himself of every opportunity to use the newspaper, the radio, to seek the public forum, to attend and speak before groups of voters. He must create an organization that will help him in these activities and that will represent him at affairs which he cannot attend.

Communication and Organization

Communication and organization . . . the first is an important set of tools, the second is the team of craftsmen that employs these tools in constructing the image you wish created.

Yet, building the proper image, selling yourself convincingly as the best candidate, is doing only half the job. Once this is done, an equally important task is to motivate the voter to cast his ballot.

History is replete with examples of situations in which the better man, the people's choice, did not win the election. This is true at all levels of government. The individual voter's complacency; his feeling that he is but one voter among many; that his candidate will win with or without his vote—these attitudes have often given the opponent just enough edge to win. The political axiom that bad public officials are elected by good people who fail to go to the polls, often has been borne out in fact. It becomes apparent that one of your organization's primary functions is getting the voter to the polls.

Getting down to more of the specifics, we must recognize two major types of campaign: that controlled by the professional political organization, and that conducted by the independent candidate.

We cannot be too concerned with the former. Here the candidate has very little to do with the operation of the program. It is handled efficiently and professionally for him, by experts who know all the techniques. Much can be learned by watching their organization in action. The most significant lesson for the independent candidate is that the professional organization always establishes a rapport with the people.

Assuming you are an independent candidate running against another independent, or even an organization-sponsored opponent, what must you do to wage a successful campaign? Consider some of these techniques:

Form Citizens Committee

1. Develop a policy committee which, under your supervision, has overall control of the campaign. This committee helps the candidate with procedures, administers the campaign, and is in charge of subcommittees.

In selecting your policy committee draw from the ranks of community leaders. Being connected with successful, well-known people is an important part of your public image. The leaders you select will be able to bring in, through their contacts, additional volunteer workers for your campaign.

2. Through discussion and conference with your policy committee, develop, outline and finalize a definite platform. Stick with it! It is imperative to maintain a consistent viewpoint. I often tell a candidate that inconsistency is the most vulnerable spot in his armor. This is a weakness resulting from the candidate's desire to be all things to all people. It is a weakness that your opponent will be quick to find and exploit. Establish the image, a reputation, a philosophy. Base it, of course, on a sincere desire to benefit the majority. Then, sink or swim, stick with it.

3. Be sure all major addresses are written out, duplicated and issued to the press. The policy committee should appoint a public relations chairman to attend all meetings at which the candidate will speak, and to distribute copies of speeches to reporters covering these sessions. This ingratiates

the candidate with the newsmen, who are relieved of the work of taking voluminous notes. More important, the actual transcript of your speech, given to the press, diminishes the possibility of your being misquoted, or quoted out of context.

4. Form a "citizens committee" under the supervision of your policy committee, drawn from friends, neighbors, relatives and other supporters. They should be prepared to devote their time and energies in carrying your message to the voter. As such, they must be thoroughly schooled in every facet of your program; and must be able to convey your philosophies and attitudes and to express your program intelligently. The "citizens committee" is your army of doorbell ringers. Members will buttonhole one voter or speak before a group. They are constantly on the firing line. They comprise the regiment that often can win the battle for you. Nothing is more effective—including a costly TV campaign—in getting the vote, than a hard-working corps of doorbell ringers.

5. Prepare a budget to cover the printing of campaign materials. This literature should be carefully planned and created under the supervision of your policy committee, and should meet certain standards.

A. Be concise in your message. If you can't say it in three short paragraphs, forget it. People will not wade through a lengthy dissertation on politics —a subject to which, unfortunately, the average voter is apathetic.

Forget the Smears

B. Do not use smear tactics! Present your viewpoints positively. Forget your opponent even exists. The voter will choose you for what you are and not for what you tell him your opponent is not. Smear literature most often back-fires. It is a poor way to conduct a campaign.

C. See that all of your printed material—your letterheads, postcards, brochures, posters, campaign buttons—is prepared by professional creative

Well designed political brochures and bumper stickers for cars are an important part of a political campaign.

people. Remember, these printed tools reflect your personality, tastes and judgment. You are better served by fewer materials professionally prepared, than by large quantities that are tasteless and ineffectual.

The importance of details

D. Finally, if you are interested at all in the labor vote, be sure that all of your literature bears a union label.

6. Purchase as much billboard space as your budget will permit. Plan your program so that your

Post cards with the candidate's picture on the front and a request to vote for the candidate on the back should be printed and given to all political workers to sign and send to their personal friends.

outdoor posters are strategically located. If you are posting such signs on private property, be sure you get a release from the owner.

7. Feed publicity releases to the press, radio and TV constantly. Think "press." That is, consider everything you do, say, or participate in as possible material for press coverage. Not all you submit will be accepted. Not all will be considered newsworthy. But every campaign warrants a certain amount of press coverage and the candidate who keeps a

Target for Contributions

Non-Partisan Norwegian - American Business Men's Committee
To Elect DANIEL J. LEADEY Mayor
77 WEST CHICAGO AVENUE
WILTON 2, IDAHO

STEERING COMMITTEE:
JOSEPH NATLAR JR

COMMITTEE TO ELECT **NOMSON** PRESIDENT—COUNTY BOARD
303 SOUTH TOWN STREET · COOK CENTER · NEBRASKA · WILson 2-3963
For additional information:
For Release:

young democrats of delaware
HARRISON HOTEL
DEMING 60, DELAWARE
Phone HAncock 3-0580

PRESIDENT
MICHAEL GIBSON
1ST VICE PRESIDENT
GERALD HARTENBERGER
2ND VICE PRESIDENT
LOUIS HEWITT
EXECUTIVE DIRECTOR
EDWIN A. MOLL

CAMPAIGN COMMITTEE
FOR THE ELECTION OF
AMOS D. CRANDALL, JR.
For Judge of the Superior Court of Cook County
WILFRED ORN - SECRETARY
13 N. LaSALLE – CHICAGO 2, ILLINOIS
RICHARD L. CLAYTON - COORDINATOR

CHAIRMEN –
COMMITTEE MEMBERS
FRANK L. CNOTTL

Political stationery should be attractively designed and also list the names of the candidate's supporters and political workers.

continuous flow of releases channeled to the communications media, even if only by sheer weight of material, is going to get more publicity. Cover the press and you're farther ahead than the man who waits to have the press cover him.

On the same subject—make sure that your releases are professionally written, that they follow the accepted journalistic style, and that they are concise. Ambiguous, lengthy political releases are all too often thrown away.

8. Set aside a certain amount of your budget for donations. The moment you announce your inten-

12th Senatorial District

DEMOCRATIC

FOR PRESIDENT OF THE UNITED STATES
LYNDON B. JOHNSON

FOR VICE-PRESIDENT OF THE UNITED STATES
HUBERT H. HUMPHREY

FOR GOVERNOR
OTTO KERNER

FOR LIEUTENANT GOVERNOR
SAMUEL H. SHAPIRO

FOR SECRETARY OF STATE
PAUL POWELL

FOR AUDITOR OF PUBLIC ACCOUNTS
MICHAEL J. HOWLETT

FOR ATTORNEY GENERAL
WILLIAM G. CLARK

FOR TRUSTEES OF THE UNIVERSITY OF ILLINOIS
(Vote for Three)
HOWARD W. CLEMENT
THEODORE A. JONES
HAROLD POGUE

FOR REPRESENTATIVE IN CONGRESS
JOHN C. KLUCZYNSKI

VALENTINE JANICKI
VINCENT D. GARRITY
EARL E. STRAYHORN

5th Congressional District

REPUBLICAN

FOR PRESIDENT OF THE UNITED STATES
BARRY M. GOLDWATER

FOR VICE-PRESIDENT OF THE UNITED STATES
WILLIAM E. MILLER

FOR GOVERNOR
CHARLES H. PERCY

FOR LIEUTENANT GOVERNOR
JOHN HENRY ALTORFER

FOR SECRETARY OF STATE
ELMER J. HOFFMAN

FOR AUDITOR OF PUBLIC ACCOUNTS
JOHN KIRBY

FOR ATTORNEY GENERAL
ELROY C. SANDQUIST, JR.

FOR TRUSTEES OF THE UNIVERSITY OF ILLINOIS
(Vote for Three)
PARK LIVINGSTON
C. ERNEST LOVEJOY
JAMES A. WEATHERLY

FOR REPRESENTATIVE IN CONGRESS
ROBERT V. KOTOWSKI

FOR STATE SENATOR
JOHN J. LANIGAN

FOR STATE'S ATTORNEY OF COOK COUNTY
JOHN H. BICKLEY, JR.

FOR RECORDER OF DEEDS OF COOK COUNTY
WALLACE S. SCHALL

FOR CLERK OF THE CIRCUIT COURT OF COOK COUNTY
EDMUND J. KUCHARSKI

FOR CORONER OF COOK COUNTY
WILLIAM T. OSMANSKI

FOR TRUSTEES OF THE METROPOLITAN SANITARY DISTRICT OF GREATER CHICAGO
ROBERT E. CRONIN
WILLIAM H. ROBINSON
GEORGE E. DOLEZAL

Election Law permits you to take this Ballot into Voting Booth, Tuesday, November 3, 1964.
Polls Open 6 A.M. - 6. P.M.

Your Polling Place Is Located At

Name.

Address.

You HAVE NOT Voted Today!

The right to vote is a great American privilege

YOUR POLLING PLACE IS LOCATED AT

and will be open until 6 P.M.

VOTE DEMOCRATIC

Democratic Precinct Committeeman (OVER)

tion of running for public office, you become a target for contributions. Many of these donations will not help your campaign directly. But your refusal to contribute can harm if someone tries to label you as uncharitable. You have to consider this as part of the cost of campaigning.

9. Form a legal section. Have legal counsel available at all times and particularly on the day of election. Become versed in election law. Be sure your staff is well aware of local laws governing elections.

10. Do not neglect the use of the distaff side in your campaign. Women are always dedicated, hardworking campaigners; and don't forget that the women's vote can "make or break" you when it comes time to count the ballots.

Atmosphere of Victory

11. The design of your headquarters plays an important part in boosting both the morale of your workers and your community image. It should be inspiring, stimulating and exciting. Posters and other campaign materials should be tastefully displayed. And, there should be an atmosphere of movement, accomplishment and the anticipation of victory. Be sure, however, while you're doing all this that it remains clean, orderly and professional.

12. Go out of your way to meet and talk to all your campaign workers. Shake their hands and know their names. They are the people upon whom your ultimate success or failure rests.

13. Make certain that your platform is written, and your campaign conducted, in such a way that the majority of the voters have no trouble identifying with you. Study the voters in your community; know who they are, where they work, how much money they make, and what they want.

Be sure that your projected community image appeals to the voting public.

You must have "sympathetic relationships" with the voter—go out and meet and talk to him in his own environment.

14. Be creative. Nothing more quickly catches the public's fancy than a political candidate who shows imagination, ingenuity and leadership. The public likes "idea" people. What you do, of course, must always reflect good taste, must be consistent with the high level of the office you are seeking. However, anything you do above and beyond the "tried and true" which is tastefully executed, impresses your name on the voter's mind, stimulates public opinion in your favor, and spurs the voter to go to the polls. Such events as parades, rallies and town hall meetings, effectively staged, prove to your constituents that you are creative, have initiative, have organizational ability.

Torchlight Parade

If you do stage a political event, remember that most people find politics dry and hard to swallow. Be sure you sugarcoat it. A political meeting should be flavored with entertainment, refreshments and tasteful showmanship.

In the personal experiences I have had in conducting political campaigns, I have found the voter extremely receptive to the "creative" political event. An event drawn from the pages of history stirs as much excitement today as it did originally. A balloon ascension in our jet age creates as much furor as when the balloon was first introduced. Similarly, a torchlight parade or an old-fashioned town hall meeting is certain to capture the public's imagination.

Realizing this, I developed an old-time rally idea for candidates running for office in a localized community in Chicago. We publicized the fact that we were going to stage this event in the old, traditional way; and advertised it through posters, handbills and direct mail.

The press activity was handled in three stages. Well in advance of the event the story was released, outlining the program of an old-fashioned town hall meeting, explaining its purposes and describing it in general terms. Four days prior, releases were issued providing specific details . . . the route the parade would take to the meeting, the speakers, and the band. Final details of the affair were telegramed to city editors of the metropolitan newspapers, news departments of radio and TV stations, and editors of community newspapers. Incidentally, this tool—the use of the telegram—is an excellent one for you to remember. It is a dramatic way of getting your message to, and read by, the editors who are apt to do your story the most good.

By rally time, we had established a rapport with the public and the press. The event was a resounding success; and local media gave it much attention because of its unusual "old-time slant."

This program — too ambitious for your small town? Remember, this was a community project in Chicago. The voting body involved in this election is probably no greater than the population of your town. And, yes, our ticket won.

The Matter of Timing

I have given you basic concepts and practical guidelines to follow. If some of these are familiar to you—so much the better. This indicates that you have a working knowledge of the task ahead. I have also detailed an actual public relations project which—other things being equal—could work for you as well as it did for us. Now, let us consider another important factor in the implementing of the program—the matter of timing. When is it most opportune to swing certain plans into action? What sort of calendar of events should you establish? Here is a suggested outline to follow from the time you start running for office until after the election is over:

1. As mentioned before, the initial step is the formulation of a policy committee. This was discussed earlier. Also, appoint and organize such subcommittees as the legal action department, the citizens committee and the public relations arm of your staff.

2. The first advertising project to finalize is contracting for your billboard advertising space. This should be done well in advance of the campaign by a committee appointed for this purpose.

There are a limited number of outdoor posters available to you and some of them, because of their locations, are of little value. Most of this space is sold on contract and the better billboards (in heavy traffic areas) are difficult to obtain. You will have to vie for this space not only with commercial advertisers but, more important, with other candidates. Commit this space to your use as early as possible.

Swing into Action

3. Political literature takes time to create, produce and print. Develop your program early, in keeping with your budget, and appoint a group to expedite it.

4. Work up a calendar of speaking engagements. Have a committee contact all local social, fraternal and civic organizations to schedule these appointments. Have your citizens committee arrange for teas, "coffee ands" and neighborhood political gatherings. Speak at as many of these as time will allow. Appoint other speakers to represent you at those affairs you cannot attend.

5. Swing your publicity program into action. Appoint a public relations chairman or a committee to be responsible for a continuous flow of material to local newspapers, radio and TV. For particularly significant and newsworthy events have him set up the three-point program discussed earlier—the general release, the specific-detail release, and the "call to action" release.

6. Three months prior to the election, swing your army of doorbell ringers into action. Each should be given a specific territory to cover. He should contact each voter in the area, sell the merits of the candidate, and urge the voter to go to the polls.

Army of Workers

7. Conduct a personal letter program a few weeks prior to the election. Ask your citizens com-

mittee to develop a chain-letter type of mailing in which friends and friends of friends are asked to send letters endorsing your candidacy. This is most impressive when such letters are sent under the imprinted name of the supporter (not the candidate). This printing is paid for by the candidate. Each member of the citizens committee approaches his friends and asks for as complete a mailing list as these people can provide. The necessary quantity of letterheads is then printed.

The candidate's staff types the letters. All the friend need do is supply the names and sign the letters. The staff does the actual posting to make sure that they go into the mail.

8. Three days prior to election, the citizens committee and the army of workers are called in and given final instructions. They are briefed on the laws governing election-day procedure; and are given final campaign materials.

9. Among the last-minute campaign materials that the committee should receive are door hangers which are to be hung on door knobs or at doorbells the night before the election. These "hangers" say, "Good morning. Please don't forget to vote today." They should contain a short "plug" for the candidate or his ticket and include helpful information about the location of polling places and the voting hours. Remember, you must get your voters to the polls!

10. Additional workers should be hired to stand at corners and public meeting places on election day, to distribute final campaign literature; but most important, they should channel the voters to the polls. Their presence on the street helps make the voter aware that this day is election day.

Watch, Watch, Watch!

11. On the day of the election your entire staff has two vital remaining functions. In fact, if I were to ascribe a byword to this all-important day, it would be, "Ring, ring, ring—watch, watch, watch!"

For, from the moment the polls open until the last ballot is counted, your staff's job is to *ring* voters' doorbells and to *watch* at the polls.

Offer additional services

Every voter should be contacted and urged to vote. I know of candidates who have set up chauffeur and baby-sitting services for housewives who may not have convenient transportation or have no one with whom to leave their small children.

Keep after these people. Follow up a second and third time to make sure they cast their ballots. Be persistent! Remember, and more important, your voters should remember, bad public officials are elected by good people who fail to go to the polls.

Watch, watch, watch! Be sure that all laws governing election balloting are adhered to strictly. Have your legal counsel available at a central headquarters for consultation. Be ever wary of your opponent—as I'm sure he is of you. See that your workers are at the polls and are alert to any illegal electioneering activities. Keep them there until the last ballot is counted.

12. Be prepared for victory or defeat. Have two messages ready for the press. Be gracious in defeat. Your attitudes and actions in losing are as closely watched by the public as are those of the winner. And, someday you may wish to seek public office again. Adlai Stevenson's comment in defeat will be as long remembered as any winner's victory message. He said that he felt like a boy who had stubbed his toe—it hurt too much to laugh and he was too big to cry.

You're a Winner

Win or lose, be prepared to serve refreshments to your weary army of workers. If you have lost the election, your staff will feel just as dejected as you. Yet, they have fought a valiant battle and deserve your thanks and a manifestation of your appreciation. What's more, there may be other campaign battles to fight and you will need that army again.

I am reminded of the story of the candidate who did not feel this way. The spoils, he felt, belonged only to the victor. The day of election he gathered his aides at headquarters, ushered them into a large banquet hall and said, "If I win, I'm going to treat you to the biggest, most delicious dinner you've ever eaten!"

The tables were already set. The appetizers, salads and relish dishes had been served. All that remained was to win the election.

However, early in the counting, it became apparent that things were not going well. And in a few hours the candidate was ready to concede to his opponent's landslide victory.

As he passed the banquet hall, he noticed two of his workers sitting at the table, gorging themselves.

"What are you men doing?" he asked. "I said we'd have a banquet only if I won!"

For a moment, the men kept eating in silence. Finally, one of them looked up and spoke. "To us, boss," he said with a forced smile of pride, "to us you're a winner!"

The political door-hanger is always a good promotional piece because it performs a public service—asking people to vote—at the same time it publicizes a party ticket or candidate.

BE SURE TO
VOTE
DEMOCRATIC
BE SURE TO VOTE!!

FIRE
WORKS

SCHOOL DISTRICTS

How far is your school from the people in your community? Is it a block or 20 years away? Did the school become an event in their past the day after they graduated? Did its problems, its needs and its goals become things for others to worry about?

Is it thought of as nothing more than a cold brick structure whose interior is completely strange to those on the outside? Is it considered a money-hungry monster whose appetite is never satisfied, regardless of how high taxes rise?

If it is deemed any of these things, then the school administration has done an inadequate job of public relations.

Create an atmosphere of understanding

The school is a vibrant, living thing. It should be as integral a part of the life of the community as it is of the children who attend it. It is the key to the future of America.

Yet, how many citizens—particularly those who have no children of school age—feel this way?

The attitude of indifference is not uncommon. It is a situation that confronts school administrators and boards of education all over the country.

As the population expands, as more students enter school, as more facilities are required—the problems and needs multiply.

The increase in school enrollment causes overcrowded classroom conditions and insufficient facilities. All too often it's only when this problem becomes acute that the school board bring its needs to the attention of the general public.

Not Like a Bar of Soap

An average school district approaches the problem of promoting a public referendum in either of two ways: 1. It designs a lavish brochure as part of a massive campaign to convince the community of the need for expansion of its facilities or programs; it accompanies this with last minute newspaper articles, doorbell marches by mothers in the PTA, and indoctrination of students in the hope they will influence their parents. 2. Some districts employ public relations firms which may be competent in commercial and industrial areas; however, the school district cannot be sold like a bar of soap. The promotion of a school district bond issue requires a deep understanding of the community, its problems and its attitudes.

This is a situation that demands Administrative Public Relations. The concept to keep in mind, here, is that of "community relations."

The key to the success of community relations is the establishment of close rapport between the school and the community. It is a program that requires full time, year in and year out, effort.

Let us consider the impression that a last minute campaign, by the school district, makes upon the public.

Breaks Down at the Top

I have nothing against the lavish brochure pointing up the highlights of the school district's program and detailing its needs. But, how does one answer the skeptical citizen, ignorant of the school's problems, who asks: If the school district needs money so badly, where do the funds come from to produce the expensive brochure or to hire the public relations firm?

The solution first lies in the development of a year-round public relations campaign. Secondly, a faculty member or administrator should be assigned, on a full time basis, to be in charge of the program. This person should come from within the school system, and should be familiar with the needs of the school and the attitudes of the community.

Community relations must be a continuing program of activities.

Left by the Wayside

Often, a school district's community relations program falters before it can pick up momentum, because it breaks down at the top—at the administrative level. Many school administrators find that they have little time for community relations—giving the child the finest modern teaching methods make possible is in itself a full time job. However, concentrating on the education of children at the expense of keeping their parents and the community ignorant of educational needs, often builds a wall of indifference, apathy and even antagonism.

A case in point is that of the typical large city school superintendent. Here is a man who, for the most part, must solve the problems of expanding enrollments and teacher shortages with a budget inadequate to handle either, let alone both. Compound this dilemma with the demands made upon his time and energy by groups with conflicting interests and he soon emerges a man with problems which seem impossible of solution. At the level of logic they may be akin to demanding that he create a round square. Yet if his problems are not to become increasingly critical, he must convey them vividly and candidly to his many publics. Only thus may he blunt certain antagonisms, while at the same time winning support from sincere people who tend to respect him because of his position, but may learn to admire him for his honesty.

This situation points to the necessity of continuous communication with the public. Specific programs can be implemented in order to sustain a continuous community relations campaign.

One program, always effective, offers evening courses to adults. In this instance, however, I am not speaking of the usual "adult education course." I suggest setting up classes to provide orientation in the new educational concepts employed in teaching today's youth.

Cannot Teach-Down

It has been said that the parent's most active interest in school affairs is reached during the early years of the child's schooling. Dwindling interest, some theorize, is the result of over-utilization of the parent's time with school and related activities, and that the young parent's enthusiasm decreases in direct proportion to her (or his) load of PTA work and in-school assistance. I cannot fully agree that this is the major cause of parent apathy.

Apathy can be attributed, in great part, to the fact that, as the child reaches higher grades and his work under new teaching methods becomes more complex, the parent is left by the wayside. When the sixth grader calls for help with his homework in new math—a subject with which most parents usually have had no experience—there can be little doubt that before the parent will risk losing his child's respect for not being able to do a "simple" math problem, he will profess a disinterest and lack of time for the school.

The school should set up evening courses to orient the adult in the "new" approaches to mathematics, science, history and language. These courses should be offered at either no charge or at a nominal fee. They should not extend over several months; rather the courses should be designed to make it as easy as possible for the adult to attend. Two hours, twice a week, for three weeks, should be ample time to indoctrinate the parent in the rudiments of a subject. Be careful that the courses do not overlap. Offer a three-week course in new math, then wait a month and offer a course in another subject; in this way the parents will be able to attend all courses without feeling that their leisure time is being infringed upon.

The curriculum of the adult orientation course should be carefully prepared. Remember that you are not dealing with a school child and you cannot teach-down. The adult should be given basic instruction *at his level;* the course should give the parent the information that he will need to answer his child's questions. Because education is progressive, impress on the parent that the subject will become more complex as his child advances in grade. Keep a list of the parents who attend the adult orientation courses. Then each year either send out bulletins informing them of the new concepts their children will be studying, or hold a one night "refresher" course on the subject.

There are several ways that you can make the parent aware that you are offering adult orientation courses. Items in local newspapers and magazines or a mailed announcement or brochure will bring results. The information can also be sent home with the child in a sealed envelope addressed to the parent; or the teacher can bring it up either during a parent-teacher conference or during a phone call to the parent, when feasible.

Too Old to Change?

Once the adult himself completes his formal education, his interest in learning drops considerably. He rationalizes his failure to keep up with new educational methods such as the new math by saying, "That's all right for young people to learn, but I was taught the old method, and I'm too old to change now." This attitude can be counteracted by using an older faculty member to teach the adult orientation course.

Be sure that at the end of each evening the adult leaves feeling that he has not only learned something, but that he has enjoyed himself. A coffee-and-social hour after the formal class session will accomplish this; so be sure the class is scheduled at an hour that leaves time for this activity — but don't rush the working man who doesn't get home until 6 p.m. and still has to have dinner—7:30 p.m. is usually a convenient hour to begin the class.

Adult orientation classes can make the big difference between interest and apathy.

When the parent has a grasp of his child's school work and can discuss or help him with it, education and the school are no longer remote.

Do not neglect the adults who are childless or who have no children of school age in your community relations program. These are the people who think they have no personal stake in the school or its future; and, these are the people who are most apt to vote "No" on a school issue.

The parent without a child in school usually represents a large segment of the community—a segment with which it is extremely difficult to establish rapport.

How do you stimulate this person's interest in the school?

Center of Activity

One method that can be used is to make the school building the center of community activity. Here are three ways to do this:

1. The school building is an ideal spot to hold civic and social meetings; contact community groups and offer them the use of the building. Interesting lectures and concerts will always bring in a number of people; set up a faculty committee to organize these events—money to come from the school budget, the sale of tickets or from a local organization that co-sponsors the event. Adults who make use of the school's facilities while engaging in these activities, come to know the school; and develop a warmer, more comfortable feeling toward it.

2. Adult education courses which appeal to special interests or hobbies help induce the public to

attend your school. These courses should be announced through local media, direct mailings, and word of mouth.

Another area of popular interest that the school can utilize in contacting the childless adult is the bridge club or tournament. Find a faculty member who is a bridge enthusiast and appoint him to organize this type of activity in the school building during the evening.

3. The school's vocational guidance counselors, during their regular course of bringing in business or professional men from the community, should not neglect the man who has no children in school. The school always flatters any individual who is asked to speak at a career guidance program.

Elementary schools also may bring in the business or professional man who has no children in school, by asking him to participate in a classroom program in which the course of study is in some way connected with his activities.

Vital Link Established

Encouraging faculty members to reside in the area is an effective way to improve community relations. Admittedly, this is a difficult task to accomplish, as some of the teachers living outside the area will be reluctant to move. The school administration, with the aid of the community, should make special arrangements so that it is attractive for the teacher to move into the area.

To make such relocations palatable, housing may be made available at moderate costs; or local real estate agents can offer furnished homes or apartments on a nine-month rental basis. Arrangements also can be made with local business and professional men for merchandise and service discounts to teachers who reside locally.

With the faculty residing within the community, a vital link in community relations is established.

The citizen can no longer complain that the school is trying to "push through" unnecessary bond and tax issues with the money coming out of his pockets, because those with vested interests, school administration and faculty, are now local residents too, and are paying their share.

More than this, the school administrator or faculty member who lives in the community becomes a neighbor, with the same common community problems and desires. As a resident he can now discuss school and educational problems on a personal welfare basis rather than as one with a special interest. He can help create an enlightened atmosphere and an awareness of school problems that may be difficult to develop in any other way.

Local media play an important part in a continuous community relations program.

It is the responsibility of the school representative selected as the community relations director to see that a constant flow of information reaches the press. Reports of progress, problems, personnel changes and other newsworthy events should be submitted regularly.

Avoid the tendency to submit news releases which always reflect an attitude that ". . . things couldn't be better." There seems to be a reluctance to disturb the community with problems that confront the school.

From Out of Nowhere

If the public has not previously been made aware that there *are* definite problems; and, after months of "rose colored" news articles, is informed "from out of nowhere" that there is a serious problem that must be corrected—not only will it be confused, but often it will be openly antagonistic to the school, questioning the administration and refusing to lend its support in solving the problem. On the other hand, if you begin early to inform people of imminent problems, they are forewarned when the situation becomes critical and are much more willing to lend the school their confidence and support.

Since everything that concerns the school affects the public, problems as well as accomplishments must be reported.

Feature articles in the local newspaper or magazine can be invaluable. The science teacher, for example, should be encouraged to submit an article about a project on which his class is working. To increase reader interest in this type of article, always try to include students' names and addresses.

Student articles also are useful. Under the direction of the school's community relations director or a faculty advisor, an article written by a student can do much to promote public recognition of the school.

Attracting Neighbors

Do not overlook the use of local radio and television stations in your community relations program. Every broadcasting station is required to set aside time on the air for public service announcements and programs. These programs are supported entirely by the station and have no commercial attachments—public schools qualify for use of this time. Two types of programs best suit the school's needs, first, the faculty interview involving school subjects or current events.

The second type of broadcast centers around the student, his activities and his interests; this can be conducted on an interview basis, or simply by having a student speak on the subject. Also popular are student discussion panels on current events; or quiz shows, using faculty members as moderators. I prefer the student show because it never fails to attract the parent, relative, friend and neighbor.

Sports is an activity stressed too much by most schools. I am completely in favor of using athletics as one part of a community relations program—but not to the point where it becomes "all-important" and at the expense of other school activities.

Temper your community relations program to give more weight to activities that are directly related to academic rather than sporting events.

The school should be made the showplace of academic achievement. I have listed many methods that can be used to draw the public into the school building.

While the public is in the school, be sure that corridors and classrooms display examples of student achievement.

Science exhibits, artwork and students' extracurricular projects are always of interest to visitors. They graphically display the accomplishments of the student body, reflect favorably upon the school itself, and tell the taxpayer what his school-tax dollar is buying.

Do away with closed sessions

I have indicated that there is all too often a lack of rapport between the school and its community. The major cause of this situation can be summed up in one word—distrust.

Always be completely truthful in your communications with the public.

If a school bond issue is going to raise the average taxes in the community $100 a year, let the taxpayer know. Don't tell him that his tax is being increased less than one per cent. The public should respect your honesty in presenting the truth, rather than distrust you for trying to hide a fact. This practice tends to build a tremendous amount of public confidence in the school system and its administrators; it also builds faculty respect for the school.

In keeping with this policy of complete honesty, do away with board meetings held behind closed doors. The closed door session, whatever its motives, creates skepticism and distrust. Establish an open door meeting policy, with the voter invited and encouraged to participate fully in the affairs of ***his*** school.

Without public confidence, educational expansion is almost impossible. Without public trust the school administrator fights a losing battle. The voter has the right to hear what the school has to say. More important, the public has a right to be heard. Give your community and your faculty "the floor." Listen to their suggestions and grievances without bias or preconceived opinions. Conduct public meetings in a manner which encourages a free exchange of ideas.

Establish public confidence and trust

The school, or school system, adopting this attitude will create mutual cooperation; from mutual cooperation comes mutual confidence; and from mutual confidence flows trust—the essence of successful community relations.

CREATIVITY

In my previous chapters I have offered many of the techniques that I use in Administrative Public Relations. In these chapters I have given you specific examples of public relations programs that you can adapt to your own specific situation. Some of these programs may be familiar to you, others may not. There is an old saying that, "there is nothing new under the sun—only variations on a theme." Variations on most basic themes are limited only by the scope of the individual's imagination and individual creativity.

There is little doubt that imagination and creativity are keys to success in public relations and in selling yourself **big.** The programs I have suggested are only the basics. You can take any program, expand it, adapt it, change it, or interchange it, to fit your individual needs. All you need in working out your own unique public relations campaign is a little imagination.

But, you say, some people just don't have that creative "spark."

This is true—to a point. Some people are naturally blessed with "that creative touch." But don't be depressed if you are not one of those so "blessed." It is possible to *develop* creative imagination.

There are many fine books dealing with the development of creative imagination, so I will not attempt, in one chapter, to cover the entire subject. I will try only to give you a brief background on creative thinking and a few of the principles for expanding imagination.

No Direct Relationship

Some of these principles may sound incongruous, not applicable to your situation or your creative needs. You may find yourself thinking, "What does this have to do with developing a public relations program for my PTA group or enhancing my image as an attorney?"

There is no direct relationship. In developing creative imagination, you should exercise your mental processes so as to think newer, wider, more novel vistas. And the results can be very interesting.

New concepts of broadening imagination are quite similar to the radically new physical exercises, which hardly seem to have a purpose, yet prove to be excellent body builders. And, like physical training, the more you work at developing creativity, the more proficient you become.

Let's examine some of the factors that contribute to creative imagination. One of the most important is experience. Adages that claim "there is no substitute for experience" and "experience is the best teacher" certainly apply to the acquiring of a knowledgeable background for creative imagination. It stands to reason that the older you are, the more you have traveled, the more you have read, the more people you have met, the more you can call upon actual experience in solving a specific problem.

Indoor games can play a stimulating role in developing creative imagination. If you play chess, learn to be creative — don't memorize "book moves." If you are a bridge enthusiast, use imaginative bidding occasionally—don't always play by arbitrary rules. Try to do something new or different in every game you play.

Outdoor sports also can prod creativity, if you use your imagination. Think a stroke ahead in outmaneuvering your tennis opponent. Experiment with different clubs in improving your golf game. The creative second baseman on a baseball team is successful because he constantly considers all the alternatives of the game. He tries to think—before the pitch—of every play that could possibly develop around him. If you *think* while you're doing it, any sport can be a creative exercise.

Reading, hobbies and writing are creative exercises. Be selective in your reading. Before picking up a book, question how much you may learn from it. Music, drawing, painting and sculpture all challenge the imagination. Writing is probably one of the best creative exercises. And you don't have to be a professional writer to use writing as a creative tool. All that you need to do is put on your "thinking cap" and create.

What Should You Write?

What should you write? A fictional story, verse, or the description of a personal experience? It doesn't matter what the theme is. The important point is that you are "creating." You are using your imagination. Two good writing exercises I suggest are: tear a picture out of a magazine and try to write a story around it; or, cut out cartoons and try writing your own captions or gag lines.

Creative Exercises

Obviously, the best way to develop creativity is by practicing — actually solving specific problems. Before you start on your own problems, you might like to try some general ones to see exactly how imagination works. Alex Osborn, a leading teacher of creative imagination, has an excellent list of mental "exercises."[1] Here are 12 of the best:

1. Make a note of every opportunity you have had to use your creative imagination since awakening this morning.
2. Write down at least three cases where ingenuity on your part—or on the part of one of your family or friends—either improved or saved a situation.
3. It is a cold, rainy day. Think up ten ways a child of eight could amuse himself indoors by using his imagination.
4. You are left alone with a complete stranger. List six introductory topics of conversation which would be interesting yet not controversial.
5. What uses could be made of a silk hat other than as a head covering?
6. You are the minister of a church where attendance of young people is dwindling. Describe at least six actions you might take to correct this trend.
7. Most neighborhood shopping centers attract their customers by publicizing the variety and quality of their products, plus excellent parking facilities. What other features could they offer to make themselves even more attractive to shoppers?
8. Conduct an experiment in your household. Think up a new idea to present to your family. Before presenting it list all the possible objections that might be raised. Think up an answer to each objection. Then present the idea and find out how many additional objections can be raised.

Other than Brushing Teeth

9. Suppose you are a manufacturer overstocked with tooth brushes. For what uses

[1]Reprinted with the permission of Charles Scribner's Sons from *APPLIED IMAGINATION* by Alex F. Osborn. Copyright 1953, © 1957 Charles Scribner's Sons.

(other than brushing teeth) might you try to market your surplus inventory?

10. Write down six ways in which an active imagination could improve the effectiveness of a doctor.
11. As an employer, what three questions would you ask of an applicant in order to evaluate his creative ability?
12. Describe the most annoying habit of the person closest to you. Think up six tactics to get that person to eliminate that habit.

If you limit yourself to answering these questions with pure logic, chances are you will not always obtain satisfactory solutions. Cold logic can stunt creativity. This brings us to one of the most important rules of creative imagination: no idea, no matter how absurd it may sound, should ever be overlooked. Always give voice to every thought. Strive to stay away from commonplace answers. From far-flung ideas, creative approaches to a problem are developed. Never limit your thinking!

Brain Storming

There are two basic mentalities—the prudent and judicious, which logically and analytically considers all information, then makes a decision; and the inventive, which can picture, project and produce original ideas.

Both types of minds are similar in that each uses logic and reasoning to arrive at an answer; the difference is that the creative mind arrives at a new idea instead of arriving at a decision. Also, the judicious mind is confined, whereas the creative mind is unbound.

Creative thinking can be restricted by several things; set habits, inhibitions, letting experience limit a choice of ideas, self-discouragement, and timidity.

In order to think creatively, it may be necessary for you to break down past habits which restrict your thinking. Whenever you consider a problem, let your mind run loose in seeking solutions.

There are two types of creative thinking that we will discuss in this chapter—"brain storming" and individual thinking. Brain storming is a creative business method that has come into much use—and controversy—during recent years. Some feel that it is not a valid technique for problem solving. I favor this method; the more you "creatively" discuss a problem with others, the more new ideas develop toward a solution.

Brain storming, or group thinking, is done for one primary reason—to obtain a great number of possible solutions to a given problem.

Circulate the Problem

It is not likely that individual business and professional men will be able to utilize this method effectively. However, an association, chamber of commerce, political organization, civic government committee, or any other group will find brain storming valuable for creative answers and new approaches.

I will not attempt to describe all the intricacies of conducting a brain storm session, material which demands a book all its own; I will give you a basic outline for organizing a session.

The first element for a valid brain storming session is the designation of a "group leader." Only one man should organize the session and lead the discussion.

Selection of the participants is important. I prefer to have a mixed group—that is, men and women with varying backgrounds and experiences. This gives the group a better foundation on which to work.

I find that a group with more than ten people can become unwieldy.

There also should be a secretary, someone to record the ideas. Once the session has begun, ideas come fast. It may be worth while to have two secretaries alternating in recording the ideas; or it may be helpful to record ideas on a blackboard so that everyone can visualize what has been suggested.

This practice will help to stimulate multiple ideas or new angles on a single idea.

Before the session begins, the problem under discussion should be expressed in writing—stating some of its history and including a careful definition of it, and a concise statement of the type of solution desired.

I prefer to circulate the written problem several days before the session. This gives each participant a chance to think about it, and enables him to come in with one or two ideas to start off the session.

Ideas Should Be Reviewed

The meeting should be held in a place conducive to thinking. An office with no distractions, inside or out, is ideal.

Goals should be set before the start of the session. The leader should set a rigid time limit as well as a limit on the number of suggestions. Fifty answers in 20 minutes is a reasonable goal.

A good leader stimulates thought. He should compliment those who make suggestions, but should never allow any criticism of an idea. He should encourage "wild" thinking and a quantity, rather than a quality, of ideas. He should remind the group to be on the watch for ways to improve upon ideas already suggested, and to combine ideas.

After the initial session, ideas should be reviewed and the best solutions to the problem selected. All solutions that look promising should, in turn, be brainstormed separately—thereby breaking them down into smaller, more workable ideas and specific suggestions.

Creative problem solving does not have to take place in a group session. The individual business or professional man also can train and utilize his creative imagination. To be solved successfully by the individual, however, a problem should be approached methodically. The individual should clearly write out the problem, defining it carefully and in as much detail as possible. All phases should be considered—history, other existent answers, individual business or financial limitations that might affect the situation.

The individual should then select sub-problems to be considered, these to be studied and individual targets of attention selected. After this, the individual should consider what research data might be of aid to him, and where the data might be obtained.

The next step is to think of anything that may be a solution to the problem; here is where his creative imagination comes into play. He should never discount, or alternately spend much time, considering an idea; just list it and go on to another . . . keep the ideas flowing.

Once the individual has a sizeable list—having set time and quantity goals before starting the list—he should select the ideas which he thinks best carry the answers to his problem. Next he must consider ways of testing these ideas. This also involves creative thinking, as often new testing methods must be developed. He should choose practical ways to verify his ideas, such as trying them out on friends or relatives.

Finally, he should imagine all possible contingencies, even though he has pre-tested the idea. He must consider all possible actions and reactions that may result from the selection. Only after weighing all the pros and cons can the individual make an objective and pragmatic final choice.

Using the Idea Bank

There are two practices that I have found to be extremely useful in creative thinking. The first is called an "Idea Bank." Take a box, and every time you see an article in a newspaper or magazine, a letter or direct mailing piece, or an advertisement that is creative or involves creative thinking, cut it out and save it. Before you begin to solve a problem, leaf through the "Idea Bank."

It is possible that you will find a starting point for your creative thinking.

The second is called a "Think Book," a notebook that you carry with you at all times. Anytime you have a question or see something that makes an impression on you, list it in the "Think Book." This is another excellent way to stimulate creative imagination. By the way, be sure to keep a pencil and pad of paper next to your bed. Because you are relaxed and open to thought at the times while you are asleep and after you awaken, you will find that many creative ideas will occur to you. Or, you may awaken in the middle of the night with an idea; if you don't write it down at that moment you will probably forget it by morning . . . and a good idea is lost.

. . . and maybe the "Think Book"

Creative approaches to problem solving can be utilized in all phases of public relations, whether writing a news release or sales letter, planning a promotional event, or designing an office. Always try to think not only logically but creatively. Remember: You have to do a lot of **big** thinking to be able to **sell yourself big!**

Be ready to act

TECHNIQUES of PUBLICITY

Publicity, like love, is a many splendored thing —and, like true love, sometimes awfully difficult to come by—and sometimes too easy, perhaps.

I recall the community activities center which, in common with most centers, clubs, associations, federations and what-have-you, pulsated with the constant desire to have its programs aired, via the city dailies, neighborhood weekly, an ethnic newspaper or two—by radio and television certainly. And, to a certain extent, the center's publicity schedule attained a degree of success with the placement of small items on almost a regular basis. But, oh, to rate a daily's front page! This, somehow, could never be.

Then, one disastrous evening, two teenage members of the center confronted each other in a basement washroom. One boy had a gun.

The following morning the center's fondest dreams were realized—not merely the dailies' front pages, but 84-point banner streamers, no less!

Radios all over town blared the story of a boy being shot and badly wounded in a supposedly professionally supervised center. No need to plead for a smidgeon of television time—it was there *without* the asking.

Did the center want *that* kind of publicity? Is it necessary to answer that question?

During a hastily-convened meeting of the center's directors, a member of the board, who shall be nameless, suggested that this was the other side of the publicity coin, and unfortunately the side that requires absolutely no effort at all. When we think of publicity, we think only of its constructive and pleasurable aspects—never of the ugly second side of that coin.

Our director advised that the center be content with its moderate successes in placing constructive publicity, and pray never again to merit the other kind. But how do you convert negative, destructive publicity into its more positive aspects.

That's how to gain publicity without trying—how do we achieve a satisfactory publicity program by really trying? How do you SELL YOURSELF BIG through publicity?

Publicity is the most direct phase, and the most easily evaluated, of any public relations program.

The Most Direct Phase

You don't have to guess as to whether a specific publicity effort has been successful—if your story has been printed, if it has been heard on radio, if a tape or film strip has been shown on television, the effort has been an obvious success—if not, well, try again. You have no guarantee that any story will be used by the press, but you can take measures to cut down the odds considerably.

Editors, particularly those in city neighborhoods or small towns, have received news releases in every conceivable shape and form, ranging from phone calls (by-passing the work required to commit information to paper) to elaborate and even ornate specially-printed release sheets. After all, if Abraham Lincoln could write his Gettysburg Address on a paper bag, why can't you use the same device in submitting a news item? What's wrong with scrap paper, cardboard, tissue paper—any old thing?

What's wrong is that you have to SELL YOURSELF BIG to the editor *before* he can help you SELL YOURSELF BIG to your prospective audience. What's wrong is that you can't promote your own image to the editor (who is going to determine the success of your publicity effort) unless you can convince him that you are, or represent, a going concern, be it a commercial association, community improvement group, individual store or private office.

If at all possible, use your formal letterheads, at least, on which to submit your publicity. If your volume of news is such as to warrant it, by all means have news release forms printed for that single purpose, making sure their headings contain pertinent information such as your phone number if the editor should want to call for further information. Let him know that the release is for immediate use; or if it is for future use provide him with a date. This information should be on *any* news release, whether on specially printed forms, your own stationery, or on a blank sheet of paper.

Visual Attraction

Your news release should be typewritten. Typed sheets not only give the editor a better impression of you, they are easier to read and easier to edit if he should want to avoid re-writing. Typing helps to eliminate the possibility of error in the spelling of a name, which offends the person named and embarrasses the editor. And a neatly typed sheet is *visually attractive* quite apart from its content. I've found that visual attraction is a not-unimportant item—an editor may not even realize the influence of that attraction, but it's there just the same. The attraction can be enhanced further with the use of short, snappy paragraphs. Make every sentence a paragraph if you can. To see what I mean, try tacking up two typewritten sheets on a wall—one with long, heavy paragraphs, the other with short paragraphs and lots of white space. Step back and observe both as you would works of art. You are going to find the short-paragraphed page by far the most interesting, although you may not be able to read what it says from a distance.

Hurting for Space

In this connection, I try, when possible, to limit a publicity release to one double-spaced page, which has decided advantages over a lengthy release. The editor (and the reader) tends to lose interest after the first page, unless the material is of such dynamic quality and importance as to rival a Hemingway. Since there are few, if any, Hemingways among us, let's keep our material short and to the point. This has technical advantages, too. Often an editor is hurting for space—he may want to give your organization its "airing," but other groups also are clamoring for space, and a good, objective editor does not play favorites. Also, for makeup reasons, a short news story may find itself on Page One, whereas a long item almost automatically is relegated to the inside pages, barring only the degree of its importance.

A short news story has a better chance to be printed than a long one.

Earlier, I described how I used the telegram as an attention-getting device to assure press and broadcast coverage of a political rally; this is always an effective technique. Not so effective, and not so well-received, is the phone call I mentioned a few paragraphs back, which should be only a last-resort technique—the last resort being either an on-rushing deadline or a sudden, unforeseen event involving your group. The phone call has the same disadvantages as a hand-written release, only more so. Greatly increased is the probability of error—in a name, date, address. And you are putting an extra *physical* burden on the editor—you are forcing him to do your work for you. Some editors just won't. Some editors want *your* original copy to refer to if an error has been made.

Suggest It to the Editor

Which brings me to the content of your news release. Unless you are a fairly accomplished news writer, *don't* try to follow a newspaper's traditional inverted pyramid style, in which the salient parts of the story are lumped into the first paragraph, and expanded in greater detail in succeeding paragraphs. To be sure, give the editor the who, what, when, where, why and how of your material—but he is much better equipped to take it from there. He also knows what he wants in the way of *style*, which is the matter of what is to be capitalized, what may be abbreviated, what is to be boldfaced, etc. This is the particular newspaper's own procedure, and you cannot be expected to know it.

Create neighborly interest

If you have material that you feel lends itself to "feature" treatment, you may suggest it to the editor, but again you yourself are not likely to be qualified to write it that way. When the editor agrees with your estimation, he will see to it that your material is handled as a feature story, which is more or less the opposite of a straight news item—the central point, which leads off the inverted pyramid in straight news, in a feature story becomes the climax, and the treatment of the material usually stresses human interest. As to the latter, remember that people are more important than objects and dates. Try to name as many persons as are pertinent to your story, giving some idea of why they are pertinent, and, especially for the community and rural press, their home addresses. Let a reader know that a neighbor two doors away is doing something, and the reader becomes interested. Even big city dailies and radio and television use home addresses whenever they can. *Everyone* is a localite in his own community, wherever it may happen to be.

Subject matter of your news release must contain newsworthy material.

The word "newsworthy" has been defined as "of sufficient interest to appear in newspapers" (and, by implication, the broadcast media). A release has to have news value. It must fulfill the reader's interest in what is going on about him; or it must satisfy his curiosity.

One of the best definitions of newsworthiness was uttered by John M. Shaw, an executive of A. T. &. T., when he said, "News is not what we want to tell other people, but what other people want to know about us." To SELL YOURSELF BIG keep that in mind—and keep it short.

Keep on the alert for picture possibilities.

Think of an Action

In submitting any news release, in asking the press to cover what you feel is a newsworthy event, never overlook the possibility of an accompanying picture or pictures. It is no accident that metropolitan dailies employ picture editors who do nothing but screen photographs the papers have received, and follow up on picture potentialities. Even the smallest neighborhood weekly will have a working arrangement with a local photographer to be on assignment whenever he is needed, to cover events the editor thinks may be newsworthy or at least of some value to his paper.

I am not convinced that any picture is worth a thousand words, but there is no doubt that many pictures transcend the news stories they illustrate. Although it is unlikely that your group, store or office can produce a photo with the dramatic qualities of, say, a million-dollar fire on Main Street, or a halfback scoring the winning touchdown, nevertheless, there are many ways of creating interesting pictures.

Unfortunately, some pictures, of necessity, are going to be dull. When your group holds an election, you will want a picture of the new officers to be published and, except that some readers will be interested in seeing the faces of those they may happen to know, there isn't too much you can do with such a lineup. You have your "left to right," and that's it. Still, there is much that you can do to make other pictures interesting besides including dogs, children and pretty girls. When you think of a photo, think of an *action*.

Putting Up a Tent

- A local leader wielding a shovel in a ground-breaking ceremony.
- Somebody pointing to a significant word on a blackboard.
- An arm waver.
- Someone peering up into the sky.
- A clown (or Santa Claus) entertaining your group's children's party.
- Someone standing up in the audience.
- Two people shaking hands (or one may be handing something to the other).
- Somebody embracing somebody else.
- Your Boy Scout troop putting up a tent.

Get the idea? Here, it might be worth your while to re-read the chapter on "The Use of Creativity in Public Relations." The two go together like Damon and Pythias.

Whenever you send out a photograph, be sure that you attach a caption to identify it. For example, if you send out a picture of the new officers of your association, attach a typewritten sheet to the back of the photo to the effect that ". . . These are the newly elected officers of the XYZ Association, elected at a recent meeting. . . ." Then give the names, indicating which side of the picture you are starting from—i.e., (L-R) for left to right, or "From left:"—note the office that each holds and his home town and state. Most important in photo identification: be sure that names are spelled correctly!

Better than having your own photo made for

submission to a newspaper or TV station—is to convince the editor that he should send *his* photographer to cover your story. Of course, the expense then becomes that of the newspaper, but far more important, from your viewpoint, is that the editor now has a vested interest in the picture, and is almost certain to use it in a subsequent issue, which means that your publicity effort, at least as regards the photo, is almost assuredly a success. The editor would not assign a photographer if he did not believe the picture a potential asset to his publication.

A Potential Asset

If your organization is of reasonably solid substance, it will be valuable to have ready for submission with publicity material, portrait photos of your officers. These can be anything from full 8″ by 10″ prints to those of wallet size—but be sure they are glossy, black and white, and of sharp contrast. Appropriate photos may be turned in with your publicity from time to time. Some groups go to the trouble and expense of making their own one-column engravings of portrait photos, from which "mats" may be made for newspaper use. These save the editor the cost of engravings, plus a certain amount of bother in preparing pictures for publication.

Do the Editor a Favor

An editor is always on the lookout for good, usable photos, not merely for whatever news value they may have, but for makeup purposes. Compare a newspaper page with no photos at all (if you can find one) to one with several pictures. The latter is far more interesting and appealing to the reader's eye—even when he is too far away to read the type. Again, it is a matter of attractiveness, and of creating in the viewer or reader a *desire* to buy that newspaper. So do the editor a favor, give him your publicity pictures.

Make it a practice—a habit—to submit news releases to radio and television stations as well as newspapers. Radio is being listened to as never before, and television is, of course, the most striking communications medium in the world today. In addition, broadcasting companies, when licensed, are required by law to devote a given portion of their time to public service, and your group, in common with many civic, charitable and service organizations, is entitled to some of that time.

Just as you cannot be expected to know how to write a news or feature story—so it cannot be expected that you can turn in full-fledged radio and/or television scripts with the special forms and language they require. Your news release is sufficient—if the radio or television editor is interested, he will have your story transcribed for broadcast use. For television's purposes, picture possibilities are all-important. If a TV editor likes your story enough to assign his mobile unit—the tapes, or film strips, of your activity are almost sure to show up on the electronic tube and in the homes of those you wish to reach.

Study a Paper's Needs

Know publication dates and deadlines and plan your releases accordingly. There is nothing quite as dead as the story that missed a deadline—and there is no excuse for it. Most of the time your publicity can be planned far enough in advance to give an editor plenty of opportunity to work it over and to schedule it. It is true that occasionally something happens perilously close to deadline—but if you analyze your operation properly you will see that, ninety-nine times out of a hundred, you can make solid publicity plans well ahead of any deadline.

Also, cooperate with an editor. If he should ask you to keep him informed about some project your group has undertaken—*keep him informed.*

There's many a slip 'twixt the plane and the grip. Sometimes, even with an editor's best intentions, because of space or makeup requirements or printing problems, your story is going to be left out. A polite query by phone or in a note will indicate your concern, and has an additional plus—next time the editor is apt to pay extra attention to your copy.

Try to study, if you have the time and opportunity, the *needs* of a newspaper or broadcasting organization. For example, at certain times of the year even the biggest of publications is going to have more in the way of publicity releases than it can handle—after the Summer vacation season when clubs and groups, fortified with energy and new officers, go to work in earnest, or at Christmas time when everybody and everything is in a feverish rash of parties, benefits and what-not—and all want it known through the press. True, at such times you, too, may be bursting with energy, but consider the editor's plight and treat him accordingly. Make your publicity succinct and to the point—go easy on your demands—let him know you know he's got a problem, and that you will understand it if you get left out. The probability is that you are the one who *won't* get left out.

On the other hand, during the slow Summer season, or right after New Year's, give the editor *additional* story and picture material. At these times he may be aching for copy to fill his pages. Advertising may be down and other organizations may have closed up shop temporarily. Fill the breach with as much as you can. You might start a series of articles on whatever it is your group is promoting, which then could run into the busier seasons and virtually guarantee continued space for your interest.

Make Personal Contact

Make personal contact with the editor; involve him with your organization.

The time has long passed when a newspaper or broadcast editor will freely accept a bribe—or knuckle under to the pressure of an advertiser. *Most* editors today are affected in reverse by bribe offers and advertisers' threats—such tactics may result in good publicity material *not* being used.

But that doesn't mean the editor is not a human being and not subject to the ordinaries of human life—the interchange between people—a regard for people and problems—his own civic and political interests. The editor is a human being; treat him as one. Call him, visit him, share a coffee break with him, find out what makes him tick—you may discover that you like him enough to admit him to your circle of friends! Above all, with personal contact you can learn his problems and needs—and he can learn those of your organization. You are asking him to help you by providing free newspaper space or air time—offer to help him in any way that is practicable. On those special occasions such as Christmas, place even a small greeting ad in your or your group's name—a token of your sincerity if nothing much else. He has not been bribed—you have offered no bribe; he has not been threatened with the loss of advertising revenue—you have not canceled any ads if you are an advertiser. You and he have established an atmosphere of friendliness and mutual assistance and understanding. His newspaper and your organization both benefit. You may be reasonably sure that, when space problems arise, *your* articles almost never will be omitted.

To Skin a Feline

In regard to radio and television, in particular, publicity opportunities are available through a number of "talk" shows. Some radio stations devote many hours a day to interviews with controversial personalities, with representatives of groups such as yours. A lot of time has to be filled, and radio (to a lesser extent TV) interviewers are constantly searching for interesting persons with whom to talk—in some cases bringing in the public via telephone lines. It does not take too much doing to contact these stations and arrange for your president or most articulate speaker to be interviewed. Your cost is nothing—your benefits may be incalculable.

If there are more ways than one to skin a feline, there also are many ways to involve an editor with your organization. Most obvious is, of course, the press conference, when editors, reporters and photographers are invited to meet with and interview a prominent personality, or to learn about a sensational new product. But the occasion for a *bona fide* press conference is a sometime thing, and, particularly in the neighborhood, suburb or small town, there are more numerous and far more intriguing ways to involve the press.

Probably there is not an editor (or publisher) alive who has not at one time or another been invited to serve as a judge in a beauty contest. Well, why not? An editor enjoys pulchritude as much as the next man, and meanwhile your group, sponsoring or co-sponsoring the contest, is getting its newspaper story or those TV shots of girls in bathing suits. What if the editor is a woman? There is always a cake-baking contest.

Always the Pet Parade

There is always a pet parade. Get the editor to ride his own car in the parade, with the name of his newspaper, radio or television station prominently displayed. You have gained some free publicity, but so has he. Parades and contests can be created by the dozen, and everyone from tots in buggies to the Boy Scout Bugle Corps to the local high school marching band to the civic, business and political leader is eager to get in on them.

In a more serious vein, an editor can be interested in the work your organization is accomplishing and can be induced to join your board of directors, perhaps even take a part in your organization's activities.

It has happened and will continue to happen, as many leaders of chambers of commerce, community centers, civic, welfare and improvement groups all can substantiate.

All of these "mechanics of publicity" merely scratch the surface of the possibilities. They are designed to help your group's publicity program—but they also help press outlets and the community itself.

Now it's up to you

If these ideas have only scratched the surface, so has this chapter. Many books have been written about the different techniques of news and publicity, and many more will be. I ask only that you consider these methods and expand them as a vital way to SELL YOURSELF BIG.

Editors prefer that news releases be sent to them on specially printed news release forms. Make sure that the heading contains all necessary information, such as your name and phone number. The editor might want to call you for additional information.

On the following pages are examples of what I talked about previously.

IMMEDIATE RELEASE

Information: **John Jones—LO 6-4327**

Vigorous opposition to plans that would make Main a one-way street eastbound, was voiced today by Gordon Brown, president of the Thorndale Community Council.

Presiding at a general meeting of the council in the Thorndale school, 3528 Frontage Rd., attended by some 100 persons, Brown took the occasion to lash out at "yesterday's high-handed actions of the city traffic department."

"It seems to me that the city is completely ignoring the people who live and work on Main St.," Brown said.

"One-way traffic may be desirable where traffic is congested, but there simply is no justification for it on Main St.," he declared, adding that residents would be hampered and merchants would lose business if the plan goes through.

He concluded with an appeal to Thorndale residents to make their opinions known by letter and phone to the city administration.

In this publicity release, an organization takes a stand on an issue affecting the people of its area.

How it feels about the measure, and the measure itself as well as an identification of the organization, lead off the article.

The second paragraph tells when and where the issue was discussed, indicates a certain amount of support for the group's stand, and names the "culprit."

In paragraphs 3 and 4 the organization, through its spokesman, tells why it opposes the city's plan, and the 5th paragraph urges neighbors to help the group do something about it.

FOR IMMEDIATE RELEASE

Further information: **John Jones—LO 6-4327**

"Your Tax Dollar" will be discussed by Henry Smith, director of the Civic Service League's public affairs department, during a meeting of the Thorndale Community Council at 8 p.m. Monday, June 17, in the Thorndale school, 3528 Frontage Rd.

Mr. Smith, who has been associated with the Civic League since last November, formerly served as executive secretary of the city's capital improvements division, and was instrumental in such municipal projects as the new court building and the Thorndale Freeway.

Gordon Brown, council president, invited neighbors to attend Monday's session, which is open to the public.

A question and answer period will conclude the talk, after which coffee and cake will be served.

First paragraph combines all pertinent information, and can stand by itself if a newspaper should be short of needed space.

Second paragraph gives something of the speaker's background and indicates why he is qualified to discuss the subject and why he is worth hearing.

Third paragraph is an invitation to the general public through the sponsoring group's leader (not through the newspaper).

Final paragraph contains extra inducements for the public to attend.

FOR IMMEDIATE RELEASE

For further information: **John Jones—LO 6-4327**

Photos enclosed

Maybe, as somebody once said, nice guys finish last -- but you can't prove it by Sam Connor.

Sam is a nice guy -- a real nice guy -- as anyone on Frontage Road can tell you.

He minds his own business and is known as a good neighbor. Anytime anyone on the block needs help Sam is right there to provide it -- each time with a genuine smile on his handsome Irish face.

That's probably why Sam is such a valued member of the Thorndale Community Council, which has benefitted from his earnest work these many years, and also why his Connor Service Station on Main Street is so well patronized.

Anyway, a couple of weeks ago, one of Sam's neighbors at 2719 Frontage, Mrs. Edna Clark, a widow (and a pretty one at that), got herself into something of a bind when she tried to back her car out of her garage during the icy conditions that prevailed.

Somehow, although moving slowly, the car skidded off the driveway and came to a stop alongside the white picket fence that surrounds Mrs. Clark's lawn, in such a position that to move it might have smashed the fence.

Fortunately for Mrs. Clark, Sam Connor had just stepped out of his home across the way at 2722 Frontage, and had seen the mishap.

Typically, Sam lost no time volunteering his help, which was gratefully accepted. It took nearly two hours for him to maneuver the auto away from that fence, but finally it was done with no harm to the fence or the car.

This past Sunday morning, the former Mrs. Edna Clark became the bride of Mr. Samuel Connor in ceremonies conducted by the Rev. Frank Hauser at the Thorndale Presbyterian Church.

After the nuptials, Sam confessed he had been interested in Edna for a long time. "Maybe it was the car that did it," he said, grinning happily.

The newlyweds have a problem -- one has to sell a house. Another problem has been solved -- the new Mrs. Connor has become a member of the Thorndale Community Council. "Been trying to get her to join for six months," Sam declared.

Nice guys finish last? You can't prove it by Sam Connor.

Unlike a straight news story, the point of a feature story is contained at or near the end, in this case the wedding of two neighbors. It should have elements of human interest, as against the rather cold straightforward wording of an ordinary news release.

In paragraph 4 there is a propaganda seed for the community council, as well as a "plug" for Sam's business, and the council propaganda is strengthened in the next to last paragraph, hinting that joining the community council is a good thing for anyone to do.

In submitting this material, or any other, to an editor, he should be apprised that he is at liberty to handle it in any way he desires. After all, it is *his* decision since he is responsible for what appears in his newspaper.

PUBLIC RELATIONS PITFALLS

I have tried, throughout this book, to give you a basic understanding of the underlying philosophies and practices of Administrative Public Relations. I have discussed the tools and their application.

For this book to be truly effective, however, I must point out some specific "dangers" in the development of your own public relations program. Watch for these common "pit-falls":

1. The Public Interest: All of your programs must, in one way or another, serve the public good as well as your own.

Hold on to public favor

A case in point is the opposition of the American Medical Association to "Medicare" legislation. A great number of the citizens of this country recognized that a large proportion of senior citizens were not able to afford, or obtain, adequate medical services. So widely recognized was this problem that every administration, from Dwight D. Eisenhower on, proposed varying forms of health care legislation. The A.M.A., so strongly opposed in basic philosophy to this type of legislation, found itself in the position of urging the public to work against "what the public thought was its own best interest." Through the use of an extensive public relations campaign, the A.M.A. expressed its position to the people through its members, through billboard advertising, through radio and TV spot announcements and through news stories. It urged the people to write their congressmen and request the defeat of "Medicare."

When it finally became apparent that its campaign was not succeeding, the A.M.A. drafted substitute legislation, entitled "Eldercare," and urged its passage. The futility of this attempt was obvious from the outset, as "Eldercare" was the same legislation which was introduced during the Eisenhower Administration, and which the A.M.A. had previously asked the citizens of the United States to oppose.

How to Lose Public Favor

The country now sensed that the reversal of the A.M.A.'s position and its continued opposition to health care legislation was **not serving the public's best interest.** As a result the A.M.A. campaign failed, and the public today looks at all of its promotional activities with a critical if not jaundiced eye.

2. Overexposure: Even though you are interested in obtaining recognition through public relations, excessive exposure can cause you to lose public favor, and reach a point of diminishing returns.

A major New York utility company placed, in strategic positions around construction sites, signs which explained that it was "Sorry for this inconvenience . . . this is another improvement for New York." The public reaction, at first, was excellent, and the traffic congestion caused by the construction was accepted with tolerance because of the apology. When, however, the New Yorker was faced with the same inconvenience day after day, month after month, the signs became a focus of ridicule and annoyance. Nationally known comedians now used the "New York signs" as foils for their humor. The point of diminishing returns had been reached. Each new sign was now creating ill-will. Had the utility company switched emphasis during the campaign to a new, fresher approach, it would have been able to continue to garner the favor of the people. Overexposure had destroyed an effective public relations program.

Only the New and Fresh

3. Continuity: No Administrative Public Relations program can hope to succeed without continuity. In nearly every chapter of this book, I have pointed out the importance of continuity to the overall program. The businessman was told to maintain a continuity of relationships with his customers after the initial contact. The politician was warned of the necessity of having consistency and continuity in his platform—he could not be all things to all people. The school district was advised to maintain a continuing community relations program.

Continuity is the fine thread which binds all fields together. Each must have effective and continuing relationships with its particular public.

4. Creativity: Without a creative approach, an Administrative Public Relations campaign cannot achieve its purpose. Today, so much vies for public attention, that only the new, fresh idea and approach which reflect creative thinking can hope to capture the public's imagination.

At one time, Hollywood represented the very best in creative public relations. Hollywood took ordinary people, glamorized them, surrounded them with an aura of mystery, put them on pedestals, sold them as idols, and created, through the use of every possible public relations technique, what were known as "Stars." Few visitors ever were permitted on a movie set, every possible method was used to prevent the public from knowing that the movie industry was composed of hard working, talented professional people, who were not really very glamorous when at work (or elsewhere). Premieres were the vogue. The public was dazzled by the spectacular excitement of the events. Spotlights cut through the skies. Streets were dazzlingly illuminated. Red carpets were rolled out. And huge limousines discharged glamorous film stars.

What has happened to all this Hollywood glamor? In the past 20 years, no really new approaches have been taken. No new ideas have been created. The public has become blasé to the premiere. It's just another set of spotlights, another red carpet, and another Hollywood star parading before a microphone or camera. The old excitement is gone. Hollywood has lost its creative touch.

Bound by Old Patterns

In Hollywood, public relations men come and go as fast as the new films. It is one of the least secure jobs in the industry. And yet, each new man who comes seems to be a product of Hollywood itself. Bound by old patterns and ideas, following in the footsteps of his predecessors, he brings forth little in the way of new and fresh ideas.

Hollywood's problem can be your problem, if you fail to recognize the importance of change. Continually seek new methods of exposure, and new and creative ideas which will spark the public imagination. Creativity is a vital factor in the continued success of your Administrative Public Relations program.

5. Truth: Through public relations you can create any image that you desire—keeping that image, however, is not always easy. Your Administrative Public Relations program will have little chance of success if it is not based on truth. I have said earlier that you can reflect only what

you really are. This concept is basic and unalterable. Respect the public's intelligence. A program which is based on deception soon will be exposed, with disastrous results for its proponent.

Avoid the pitfalls

Images are fragile—they shatter easily. To protect your image you must build it on a foundation of truth; embellish it with creative ideas; develop it with management consultation concepts; sustain it with continuing relationships; and project it with the finest techniques of publicity.

Hollywood premiers have lost much of their glamour because they are all alike and lack creativity.

World Wide Photo Service Picture

FUND RAISING

To speak of public relations as it applies to fund raising is to deal in a redundancy, because fund raising is practically pure public relations in and of itself. The fund raiser, whether he is a professional or volunteer, performs an act of public relations with virtually every move he makes, every word he says or writes.

Perhaps in no other field are human relationships as sensitive as in this field and for good reason. As a fund raiser, you are asking other persons to part with hard-earned dollars, for which they apparently will get nothing in return. Under this circumstance, a contributor to a charity or a cause does not require too much provocation to turn his back on whatever his interest may be. If he should feel offended, justifiably or not, by the fund raiser or the fund raising group, it is only too easy to withhold his check. Whereupon the fund raising program, in his case, collapses.

But the failure is one of public relations—you have failed to uphold an image, to sell your particular bill of goods, to retain a friend. Most of all, you have failed to SELL YOURSELF BIG.

In this era, fund raising has assumed staggering proportions. It is the third largest "industry" in America today, and perhaps in the world. For the benefit of civic, health, education, welfare, cultural, religious and many other causes and programs, residents of the United States, in 1965, parted voluntarily with more than $11,000,000,000. That is eleven *billion* dollars. Of this incredible sum, about eighty per cent came from living individuals, as distinct from the twenty cents of each dollar provided by foundations, corporations and a variety of charitable bequests.

Eleven Billion Plus

The two words, "living individuals," epitomize the oneness of fund raising with public relations. Just as small, single bricks are cemented to each other to fashion huge office or apartment buildings, so do single dollars, aided and abetted by fives and tens, accumulate into billions and into an enterprise that is literally changing the face of America.

How Many Buildings

I think it is safe to say that no American has gone untouched, if you will pardon the pun, by the fund raisers—even if he only dropped a dime or quarter into a tagger's box. That new hospital wing—a new parochial school building (on a single Sunday afternoon a few years ago a Catholic church raised no less than $350,000 from among its own parishioners for a modern, fireproof school)—a new temple sanctuary, designed by one of the country's foremost architects, the result of a $3,000,000 drive, again from among the congregation's own members.

How many medical research buildings have been erected all over the country as a result of successful fund raising efforts? How many community centers? Settlement houses? Concert halls and theaters? It might take a full-length textbook merely to list them all—and en masse they add up to a colossal monument to public relations. Even if we get away from bricks and steel, fund raising dollars account for so many things we would otherwise be without—camp outings for underprivileged children, leader dog training for the blind, pre-nursery and nursery programs, recreation for senior citizens, free classes of all kinds, the United Service Organization for servicemen away from home, food and medicine for the indigent, free cancer detection clinics—I could go on and on and still do no more than scratch the surface.

We All Contribute

In one degree or another we all contribute to this vast philanthropic structure, and at one time or another many of us may find ourselves involved as volunteer fund raisers. With that in mind, this chapter will deal with some of the pertinent facets of fund raising, always bearing in mind that it is the essence of public relations and that other chapters apply here as much or more than as, in other areas of American life.

Let us zero in on that backbone of fund raising, the individual donor. Why does he voluntarily part with a dollar, or ten, or a thousand? What is his *motivation?* What does it take to induce him to become a philanthropist? What does he want in return?

It has been said, among the fund raising fraternity, that people do not give to causes—THEY GIVE TO OTHER PEOPLE.

This I believe to be largely, though not absolutely, true. If you have done any fund raising at all, you undoubtedly have experienced that moment when one member of your committee has received a donation from a gentleman who previously had refused another member of your committee. What made the difference? Try the following for size:

1. The second, and successful, caller was a personal friend of the donor, and therefore received the "favor."

2. The second caller was known to the donor by name as a man of some standing and influence in the community, and the donation was a matter of present or future prestige for the donor.

3. The second caller was a better salesman. As in everything else, salesmanship can be the plus factor.

4. The second caller was on the prospective donor's own list of persons to be contacted for a philanthropy of his own. "You give to my cause and I'll give to yours."

5. The second caller was a stranger to the donor. This is a contradiction of the first example, yet the fact remains that some people would prefer *not* to contact friends and acquaintances—and some prefer not to be contacted by those they know.

6. The second caller knew something about the prospective donor—his preferences, his desires, his prejudices if you please—which enabled him to make the successful contact.

The Unknown Soldier

The inside story among fund raisers is that, depending on the person who does the soliciting, donations can be obtained for the widow of the Unknown Soldier. Which is almost not an exaggeration.

Built-In Apparatus

Despite the foregoing, many people *do* give to causes. If a man should lose a loved one to an incurable disease—cancer, leukemia, heart failure—he may very well devote the rest of his life and the bulk of his estate to help find a cure. Attesting to this important source of philanthropic funds are thousands of hospital plaques bearing names "in memory of", rooms, wings, elevators bearing names "in memory of"; religious institutions with not only plaques but auditoriums "in memory of;" entire community centers named after whoever is indicated by the philanthropist; gymnasiums, arenas—anything and everything in the way of public buildings.

And if the bereaved one does not have the funds to indulge this sort of burning interest, he may very well become the fund raising leader for his cause, making up with intensive work what he lacks in the way of finances.

In other ways other people display interest in

causes, although not as fervidly. If you belong to a fraternal organization, you will help it raise funds for whatever agencies, institutions and activities it may be promoting. Here you have a built-in fund raising apparatus, somewhat insular in that it appeals primarily to its own membership, to men who belong precisely because they have like interests.

Revitalized Each Year

The fund raising-public relations apparatus may be likened to a tree which begins with the seed, root and sapling; it grows to form a solid trunk from which dozens of branches, hundreds of twigs, and thousands of leaves shoot out; the tree is revitalized every year to produce more branches, more leaves.

Broadly speaking, there are two types of fund raising programs—the ongoing, permanent appeals, and the "one-shot" campaigns. The former applies to public service agencies, which are fixed parts of the American scene, while the latter is characterized by the hospital, school or church in need of a new building.

Suppose you want to organize a campaign to provide that badly needed new church building. Where and how do you start?

Fund Raising Cadre

You start with the top echelon of your church organization—with the president and other officers, with the board of trustees, with those who have shown unusual interest. A call to a meeting is the first of your public relations devices—usually a letter over the president's signature.

At that initial meeting you have a complete roster of the congregation, from which you select those members whom you and other members of the board feel have enough interest to do active work in behalf of the church. Generally, at this stage of the campaign, you are doing quite a bit of groping—you are a committee in search of a drive.

Between the selection of a fund raising cadre and the second, bigger, meeting—and hopefully with the help of a volunteer clerical staff culled from women congregants—you have worked up a set of three-by-five cards on the basis of the membership roster. These cards contain all the information that is considered pertinent—names of husband and wife, names and ages of their children, family home address and phone number, husband's type of business, business address and phone, which of the children attend or have attended the church school, which have been baptized or confirmed, or both, at this church; if possible (and it *is* possible), the family's, especially the husband's, charitable inclinations and actual giving to other causes in the community (such as the Community Fund); clubs and other organizations to which members of the family may belong, particularly dad's membership in a country club. If, the church conducts any type of fund campaign, however small, the family's performance should be recorded on that card.

If all of this seems rather mercenary, be assured that it is. But what is volunteer fund raising if not an effort to raise money? The amount raised is the one and only criterion of a drive's success or failure. More to the point, the criterion lies in *whether or not the new building becomes a reality.*

Captains and Workers

Now we are ready for the first fund raising meeting involving all who have been contacted by letter and phone. At this session the announcement is made that Mr. Smith (usually one of the more affluent and influential members) has been named chairman of the campaign, with two, three or half a dozen co-chairmen. Those who agree to serve become "captains," who are asked to recruit "workers," the latter being personal contacts of the captains among other congregants. Depending on the size of the congregation, one or more "evaluating" sessions then are scheduled.

Here we bring into play all of those three-by-five cards so carefully worked up at the beginning. An evaluating session is nothing more nor less than an attempt to assess the individual's—and eventually the congregation's—capacity and desire to give.

Double Standard

Sometimes in campaigns of this kind, two money figures are placed on each card of a member—the amount it is thought he *can* give, and the amount it is estimated he *will* give. During an evaluating session, as many cards as possible are assessed, and ratings are given to each member as regards the value of his home, his position (owner or high official) in his business (or professional standing as a doctor, lawyer, dentist); the amounts he gives to other causes; the degree of his interest in the church (some people belong to churches and other groups for social reasons, for business reasons, because of what they may wish their children to learn and, of course, for genuinely religious reasons; some may belong to this church because they like the pastor as opposed to the pastor of another church of the same denomination).

Years of membership may be a factor; certainly the degree of activity in church affairs is taken into account; a man may be assessed high because of the number and length of his Florida vacations, Caribbean cruises or European tours.

The Pledge Blank

With workers (each captain also is a worker) selected, cards evaluated and accepted by the workers, the campaign now begins, permeated with every possible device in the public relations book. Announcement of the campaign and its purpose is made in the newspapers and broadcast media and letters of announcement are written and mailed to the church membership. Following these letters, captains and workers begin their calls of solicitation, in many cases following up with letters of their own on their own stationery. There is not, or should not be, any attempt to high-pressure congregants, for this technique could sour the most generous donor. Instead, remember that things generally even up in the long run—for every member whose contribution is considered too low, another may come up with an unusually generous donation. In some hardship cases, a congregant is not even approached for a donation.

The typical one-shot campaign is built around pledge blanks indicating gifts on a three- or five-year basis, pro-rated accordingly. There always are a number, sometimes a great number, of gifts given in full on the spot, but most will be of several years' duration curtailing future and regular billings by the church office. Money that is turned in must be acknowledged with receipts to the donors—receipts carry "thank you" messages as well as the information that "your contribution is tax deductible."

Despite the volunteer aspect of the campaign thus far, some money has to be spent in order to make it. Letters and mailings to the general congregation, pictures for the newspapers, lunches and dinners for the various committee meetings, are matters for which workers cannot be expected to pay. All of this comes off the top of the fund raising campaign itself.

Big Gifts Exploitable

Along the way, you undoubtedly will have received some gifts of unusual proportion from among the more affluent members of the church. Pending a donor's permission, which *always* should be obtained, such gifts are exploitable not only among the congregation but in the public press. Sometimes they generate other gifts of like proportion or at least some increased gifts by members who may be impressed, or even shamed, by what others have done for their church.

If ever you have thought that fund raising and public relations are separate entities, you will be disabused immediately after the campaign gets into high gear, because that is when you must call into play every public relations resource at your disposal—all of the creativity, technical proficiency, administrative skill and attention to detail that you and your fellow campaign leaders can muster.

Having announced your goal, which because of a certain amount of anticipated attrition should be higher than your actual need, you may, at the height of the campaign, engage the services of an architect, the finest you can obtain according to availability and the financial status of the fund drive.

Architect's Sketches

When the architect has prepared sketches of the new building, he should be the honored guest at a public dinner where he will display those sketches and discuss his ideas as to what sort of a building your church should have.

With him on the podium will be the pastor, the congregation president, the fund raising chairman, and anyone else considered worthy of the spotlight —the mayor of the town if you can get him, a civic leader, or any other important personnage.

This occasion is ideal for obtaining more and better gifts, it is ideal for announcing some of the really big donations received, even if they have already been announced; it is ideal for heaping more enthusiasm onto what already has been generated, thereby reinforcing the drive at midpoint and propelling it to a triumphant conclusion.

Appeal to Pride

The architect's sketches, in keeping with the essence of public relations, will be revealed not only to those who attend the dinner, but they will be circulated among the congregation and more widely through the press and broadcast media. As a community improvement, the new building is a legitimate news source, but perhaps of more importance is the effect publicity will have upon your own congregants who are footing the bill. These are the "insiders," those who are in on the campaign and the new building. Most of them will feel that their personal stature is enhanced because "outsiders" are being made aware of something the congregants have known for a long time.

In measure, we have returned to the question of what motivates a person to give to a cause. Pride, vanity, a desire for status, religious beliefs or civic interest, true altruism, and many other personal motives can be a fund raiser's vehicle.

Get the right person to solicit an individual for a donation.

Make It Short

The campaign we have just conducted may or may not be concluded by now. Ideally, it should be. The best fund raising drives are the shortest, not only because extra expenses are averted, but because the people you are soliciting may become tired of, or bored with, the campaign if it drags out too long. If this happens, your chances of obtaining a goal are diminished. I will not attempt to indicate a specific duration for any campaign; it depends too much on particular circumstances, specific needs and individual resources. But, in general, my advice is to keep it as short as possible. When it is over, be sure you give appropriate recognition to those who did the work and to those whose contributions made the new building possible. This can be done by certificates, letters of appreciation, or any other original method your committee might think up.

Along the Same Lines

At the conclusion of the campaign, the three-by-five cards with all that pertinent information—those priceless cards that served as the "guts" of your drive—should be carefully filed away. In some later year a new church administration may find it necessary to go into another fund effort, for which the precious cards will provide another "seed." Also to be stored and kept are all the other campaign memorabilia—letters, announcements, clippings, reminder cards, photos, editorials, sermons. There is always tomorrow.

That there is always tomorrow especially applies to the ongoing, permanent fund raising campaign, in which tomorrow is an important part of today in that this year's giver is counted upon as next year's giver as well, and the following year and so on. Naturally, over the years this pattern will vary and fluctuate. Some donors will lose interest in your particular cause and will be replaced by others who become interested. Death will take some, business reverses may cut down the donation of one individual, but another individual's business success may make up for it.

Some by Letter

Basically, the ongoing campaign is organized along the same lines as the one-shot. Again, cards of prospective and actual donors provide the organizational heart of the drive, the difference being that these cards contain a year-by-year record of an individual's donations only for your cause.

The ongoing campaign is not likely to be associated with a specific building, program or activity, but with the permanent raison d'etre of the institution. Any non-profit, public service enterprise may have its own fund raising pattern, despite the fact they may be getting income from a Community Fund or yearly welfare drive of one kind or another —or from a parent fraternal organization.

In such cases there is usually a paid staff, its size depending upon the size and needs of the program. The same procedure is followed year after year so that interested donors know what to expect and are prepared to give.

Ongoing fund raising utilizes as many of the set techniques as are feasible. A worker may take a list of twelve or fifteen names of people with whom he is quite close, soliciting these people by way of personal letters on his own stationery. Other workers will use the phone—sometimes it takes a half-dozen calls to obtain the gift. Dinners may be held for different segments of interested prospects—at each one a speaker is heard who represents the institution, tells about its work and its needs, and explaining that only lack of funds prevents the program from being more efficient and extensive.

At such dinners pledge blanks, to be filled out by donors, are passed out to all who attend. Even blank checks may be available. Literature of the charitable or service institution is given to each dinner attendant to be taken home and studied. Such dinners, lunches or brunches, depending on the group's preferences, not only raise money for the cause, they increase enthusiasm (just as did the architect for the church building) and bring forth more and better giving.

The fund raiser, professional or volunteer, will often make personal visits to key people of the organization—keys being those in the upper financial brackets and those of civic and social standing in the community. An interested community leader is the world's greatest fund raiser because the people he approaches and contacts know he has no vested interest in the cause.

The Tax Aspect

A community leader who is wealthy and interested in your cause is a prime source of funds, and here let us delve briefly into the tax aspects of fund raising.

Very often a gift of thousands to a non-profit organization costs the donor only a matter of a few hundreds. While I don't intend to go into detail on this phase of fund raising, it is nevertheless a fact that, because of our tax laws, philanthropy is not nearly as costly to the big givers as it might appear on the surface. Fund raisers also know that a gift of a thousand from one man may very well be less painful to him than a gift of five or ten dollars from someone less well situated financially.

There is something else you should take into consideration . . . the small gift as against the large gift!

It costs no more to raise a thousand dollars than it does to raise one or five. Indeed, the cost remains fixed no matter how large the gift.

Cost Is the Same

A letter or a phone call to a five dollar giver costs as much as to a ten-thousand dollar donor. The cost of a pledge blank is the same no matter who signs it or for how much. Similarly the cost of a dinner. Purists may argue that sometimes it is necessary to wine and dine a big giver far more than the less affluent—yet, strangely, it is usually the big giver, the noted philanthropist, who is most aware of costs, and who will insist that expenditures be cut down so that the cause obtains maximum benefits.

In describing the organization of a fund raising campaign, I touched briefly on the involvement of an organization's leaders. You might think that such men would be the first to respond to the call, yet such is not always, nor perhaps even often, the case. Too many members of a charity or service group's board of directors have the feeling or attitude that fund raising is not for them—they feel it is beneath them; something to be pushed to the background; an appeal to non-idealistic, mercenary instincts.

The Prime Source

Too many refuse to acknowledge that, without the fund raising, the organization, the cause, will collapse with alarming suddenness. If voluntary fund raising is changing the face of America, the lack of it could drastically affect our progress in the wrong way. No governmental budget, city, state or national, could fill the gap if eleven billion dollars suddenly disappeared. Like it or not, fund raising is here to stay!

The prime source of a campaign, if not the money itself, must be the group's top leadership —and this leadership must be made aware of the meaning and intent of fund raising.

To Get Things Done

Like the low repute in which the idea of publicity, press agentry and public relations was held in past years—so is today's idea of fund raising. Thus, you must sell your board of directors first, then ask them to help sell the general membership and the public. Here you bring into play everything you know about constructive and creative public relations. You don't schedule a luncheon at a hot dog "joint," but at one of the better restaurants in the community. You don't invite beatnik speakers, but the most prestigious you can get.

You don't visit a member of the board wearing sweater and slacks; you wear a conservative business suit. Volunteer or otherwise, you are part of a truly big business, and it must be conducted accordingly.

Your propaganda to the board member, and beyond him to the public, must convince him of the necessity to raise funds so that the program may go on—so that the community may benefit. Money is not a dirty word in his private enterprise. Why should it be in a public enterprise?

Your board of directors is likely to be comprised of civic, business and political leaders of your community. This is the type of person a worthy organization attracts, the type who is likely to get things done. If your board is not wholeheartedly behind your fund raising, your effort is badly crippled right at the beginning, and the rest of your campaign suffers proportionately.

Even though it is not yourself, but a cause that you are selling, you must still SELL YOURSELF BIG, beginning with your own board of directors. If you SELL YOURSELF BIG, you sell the cause big. It is that simple.

Donor Has a Chance

To this point I have discussed direct fund solicitation. There are other ways of raising money which may require more effort and extra expenditure. The single advantage is that they are possibly less painful to the donor.

A good example is the charity raffle. Hundreds, perhaps thousands of "salesmen"—men, women, children—go to work on a project of this sort, selling tickets at ten cents or twenty-five cents or a dollar—the tickets bearing the legend "donation."

Since the donor has a chance, however infinitesimal, to win something for his dime or dollar, it is an added inducement to give to the cause, although he is likely to be very objectively aware that he is still merely making a charitable donation.

The scope of the raffle-selling campaign and the value of the prizes to be won depend on the amount of money to be raised. In big raffle programs, grand prizes may be a Cadillac, or an all-expenses paid trip for two to Europe, with secondary prizes such as television sets, fur stoles and other items, or just plain cash. Secondary prizes tell the donor that his chances are not limited to one big windfall, but to a number so that his prospects of winning *something* are better. Of course, if a hundred thousand, or a million, tickets are sold for a particular raffle—how good *can* your chances be?

Nevertheless, it is understood that you have not purchased a chance, but have made a donation to a worthy cause.

Raffles cannot be publicized through the mails, as Uncle Sam takes a dim view of lotteries. This means that a newspaper story cannot publicize the word "raffle" unless the particular publication has no mail circulation whatsoever. If you want newspaper publicity, you must bring certain words into play, such as "event," "contest," or "judging." However, the average reader is virtually certain to know what you're talking about.

There's Still Time

Big raffles usually wind up with a culminating affair—at which more raffle tickets can be sold "while there's still time." If the event is being held in a community of some size, entertainers who happen to be in town for various appearances are invited to perform, free of charge, and many of them do—an inducement for neighbors to attend. Another inducement is that admission is free.

Little Old Lady

After everyone has heard the necessary speeches and you have run the gamut of entertainers, the evening is climaxed with the selection of the winning tickets, all of which are in a revolving barrel of some type. Tickets should be pulled by either reputable residents of the community or by children, possibly blindfolded so that there can be no hint or suspicion of "foul play."

As a follow-up to the raffle, winners should be publicized with both pictures and newspaper stories. If you are fortunate enough to have a winner who is a little old lady who never traveled more than 20 miles from home—and who now has a chance to see Europe—you have the makings of a good feature story which will attract news media. You may be fortunate in another way. If the winner is a wealthy member of the community, he may very well donate all or part of his winnings, or the cash value thereof, to your charitable cause. Paradoxically, cold-bloodedly if you please, a fund raiser does not like to see needy persons win big prizes. His goal is the dollar and nothing else, and through it possibly a better life for many other needy persons.

Theater parties, group tours (packaged to include transportation, hotels, sight-seeing and other features), home talent shows, dances and dinners, carnivals—you name it, almost anything is a fit subject for a fund raising program. However, as indicated, all of this involves more time, trouble, work and expense—but it is also generally more interesting to prospective donors, who may enjoy themselves while giving away their money.

A Rule of Thumb

As a rule of thumb, the more people you have involved in the actual soliciting of money, or selling of tickets, the more successful your fund raising will be. We return to the tree and its many branches and myriad leaves. The farther out you reach, the broader the base of your appeal, the more dollars will be reaped. In every action you make, every person you see or talk to, every letter or card you mail, you are grappling with a public relations problem.

Fund raising is a person-to-person affair, with specific goals and specific services, institutions and projects.

You are putting your best foot forward, aiming to please, because you have nothing else to sell save the attractiveness of your program, for which you are the advance man.

The much-maligned so-called "book of life" (there may be other names for it) is a public relations device which may be good or bad public relations depending on who is looking at it and why. What is the "book of life"? It is a yearly publication put out by some charitable groups, listing donors *and amounts* of their donations for each year, without necessarily asking permission to publish this information.

Book of Life

When these books first began to be printed and circulated, there was tremendous opposition from some of the people listed in it; most of them thought the book was "blackmail" of a sort. Perhaps it was, and is, but the books became centers of attention and the subject of much backroom perusal. Those organizations that responded to the pressure of having the books discontinued, discovered in ensuing years that the level of giving had dropped. When the books were re-instated, the level rose once again.

I won't go into the ethical aspects of such books. They are a public relations-fund raising device aimed at precisely what the charitable organization aims for—the dollar. Obviously they are effective. The man who looks at someone else's level of giving and feels shame at his own, will up his contributions in future years. People who may *not* find themselves listed will also join the roster of supporters of the organization. These books appeal to pride, vanity and everything else we discussed earlier.

A more orthodox public relations device is the house organ or organizational newspaper, generally printed in precisely the same way that ordinary newspapers are put together and on ordinary newsprint.

Like Any Newspaper

For this you need an editor who will proceed just as he would with any community or metropolitan publication. He will gather pictures of persons prominent in your drive, write up biographical news stories about them, publish photos taken at various committee meetings, feature your main speaker and/or entertainer at your culminating affair, describe the progress of the drive—and circulate it among membership and the interested public.

Page layouts, headlines, typesetting, engravings and total production, including presswork, are handled by commercial firms; they also handle more elaborate pieces made up for the campaign—house organs on magazine stock, brochures and the like.

Wheel of the Rotary

In another chapter I went into the matter of a printed emblem or symbol characterizing a commercial firm. This logo should also be designed for a non-profit charitable or service organization as a picture of the institution's image, to be used wherever feasible in publications, mailing pieces and literature created and circulated by the particular group.

Such a symbol serves two purposes—to provide a readily recognizable image that immediately identifies the organization, and to provide a sense of continuity. Year after year the symbol is there, and soon the public comes to know it, to expect it, and to feel a sense of familiarity with it. All of which helps immeasurably when your organization goes after funds.

Some emblems lend themselves very naturally to the names of groups. Witness the red cross of the American Red Cross, or the heart of the Heart Association.

Exploring the Ways

Easily recognizable, because you've seen it so often, is the two cross-bar cross of the Easter Seal which raises funds to fight tuberculosis. The wheel of the Rotary Clubs and the handicapped child of the March of Dimes have been seen and recognized by just about everyone.

Whatever your symbol may happen to be, it must be unique. It denotes your organization, and only your organization. It is your cause, the rallying point about which your activities and your fund raising revolve, it is your entire public relations program structure.

A word about creativity. To my way of thinking creativity is the most important aspect of public relations—doubly so in fund raising.

In your fund raising effort you approach hundreds and even thousands of men and women. It is up to you and your committee to find the common ground on which all of these men and women can band together for the benefit of your organization. It is also up to you to explore ways and means of appealing to widely differing individuals and widely differing groups of individuals. Creative public relations can help solve what otherwise may be a knotty problem.

Men and women have differing tastes and interests, of course, and it is comparatively easy to intrigue either. Where a woman will be attracted to a fashion show, a man will lean strongly toward that golf outing or attendance at a hockey or football game.

Most women would rather watch a cooking demonstration than a sporting goods show; with men, it is just the other way around.

However, when it comes to dealing with men of individualized inclinations, it is another story and the degree of your creativity will be a factor which will make or break your fund raising campaign.

Jazz and Beethoven

You must satisfy both the man who prefers baseball and the one who would rather play a game of duplicate bridge; he who likes modern jazz and the Mozart or Beethoven aficionado. Individualized preferences also apply to women. It is the rare fund raiser who can satisfy a multitude of tastes. Yet, as a volunteer fund raiser it is up to you to resolve such diversified interests making the degree of your creativity the determining factor of your fund raising success.

Your professional fund raiser is not a fund raiser at all. He is a fund raising *organizer* and a fund raising *administrator*. He is probably a public relations expert even if he doesn't know it or recognize it. Your professional fund raiser almost never dares to raise funds himself. *You* are the one who does it for him.

He'll Get Job Done

Am I saying that the fund raiser should be abolished as an unnecessary adjunct to your program? Not at all. In the last analysis, *he* is the one who is going to get the job done—but *you* are the one who is going to raise money.

The so-called fund raiser cannot go to the community's leaders with any kind of a direct appeal for donations. You can. The fund raiser does not have the kind of social and business relationships that allow him to rub shoulders with the influential and affluent. You and your committee do.

There are exceptions, of course. But just as you try to pick the right man to talk to a prospective donor, so must you pass over the professional fund raiser *as a fund raiser*. Ninety-nine per cent of all charitable dollars are gleaned by amateurs.

Yet, without the fund raiser's organizational and administrative ability, his know-how, his sense of public relations, you could very well close up shop. He is selling himself big but he is also helping you to SELL YOURSELF BIG.

GLOSSARY

Administrative Public Relations—Edwin A. Moll's new and unique concept which combines the best of management consulting procedures with a working knowledge of public relations. It accepts and applies psychological and sociological techniques. It utilizes all established methods of publicity. It understands the tried and true value of "Ballyhoo." It makes use of every principle of creativity, and it applies all of these practices on an individual basis to fit the specific needs of any problem, by creating and presenting a public image based on truth.

Advertising — Paid messages to a public through media such as newspapers, magazines, radio, T.V., billboards and point-of-purchase displays and posters. In Administrative Public Relations, the basic difference between advertising and publicity is that publicity is not paid for and advertising is.

Attitude—The feelings of an individual or group toward a particular situation or action. A politician must have a sympathetic attitude toward the wants and needs of the majority of voters he represents.

Climate of Awareness—A concept coined by Edwin A. Moll to describe the efforts of an association to focus the public's attention upon the profession or industry which it represents.

Communications—To transmit or exchange ideas and information in direct and indirect relationships. The public school must communicate with the voting public to build up an awareness of educational needs.

Community Climate—The receptivity of a community toward an idea or image which is being presented.

Community Image—The image that a community or municipality presents to both non-residents and to residents.

Continuing Communications — Communications should not be a "one-time" attempt; to be effective it must be a continuing program. It is not enough for the accountant to be with his client only once a year at income tax time—he should be in constant communication through newsletters and personal letters to keep the client aware of the services that he and his profession can offer.

Continuing Relationships—Keeping in constant contact with a public. The merchant should have Continuing Relationships with his customers to keep them aware of goods and services that he offers.

Continuity—An uninterrupted succession. Administrative Public Relations programs should be developed and presented in a planned sequence. This is also true of publicity, where there should be a logical progression from press releases to promotional devices to follow-up stories, etc.

Creativity—To bring a new idea or method into existence. The ability to create something rather than to imitate. Every aspect of Administrative Public Relations should be approached creatively, looking for new and different ideas to add to an existing operation.

Exposure—To lay open to public view. In Administrative Public Relations the degree to which an individual, organization or municipality comes into contact with various publics through press media or personal effort.

Feature—Story where the main element is human interest rather than spot news.

Image—In Administrative Public Relations an image is the total awareness, understanding and impression that is created and presented by an individual, organization or a municipality to a designated public or publics.

Initial Contact—An important basic concept in Administrative Public Relations. The first impression that an individual, a business, a practice or an organization makes on the people being served. The *initial contact* that a patient has with a doctor is the atmosphere created by office decor, and the attitudes of the receptionist and the doctor.

Overexposure—To present for too long a time. It is possible, in Administrative Public Relations, to become overbearing in a program or campaign and ruin the basic image that is being presented.

Project—To present, cast forward, or to communicate with a prescribed audience. A political candidate projects an image to his public.

Publicity—Actions or devices designed to attract public interest; the dissemination of information of news value issued to gain public attention or support; issuance of information or promotional material. Publicity is only one phase of Administrative Public Relations. Only after the internal image has been perfected can publicity be used successfully to attract public attention.

Public(s)—The community, or people in general. In Administrative Public Relations the word is used to identify people grouped together for a common purpose: (for example) the reading public, in newspapers or magazines.

A businessman may deal with several publics or groups — his customers, his friends, his employees and his colleagues.

Reciprocal Arrangement — Combining the public relations efforts of two stores whose operations complement each other.

Reflection—Throwing back an image. The reflection of an association's members to the general public is evidenced in the image that the association creates and projects.

Space—Used in advertising to denote an amount of coverage purchased in printed media.

The Public Good — In the best interests or welfare of the public. The promotional efforts of an association should be centered around presenting information "in the public good" to aid people in daily living.

Time—Used in connection with radio and TV to denote the duration of a broadcast. A radio station, for example, may give time, as a public service, to a non-profit organization, to broadcast a public information message or program.